Quiet Talks
on
Prayer

Quiet Talks
on
Prayer

S. D.
GORDON

BARBOUR
PUBLISHING

© 2013 by Barbour Publishing, Inc.

Editorial assistance by Jill Jones.

Print ISBN 978-1-62836-665-5

eBook Editions:
Adobe Digital Edition (.epub) 978-1-63058-127-5
Kindle and MobiPocket Edition (.prc) 978-1-63058-128-2

Published by Barbour Publishing, Inc., P.O. Box 719,
Uhrichsville, Ohio 44683, www.barbourbooks.com

*Our mission is to publish and distribute inspirational products
offering exceptional value and biblical encouragement to the masses.*

Member of the
Evangelical Christian
Publishers Association

Printed in China.

Contents

Introduction

Everybody wants to pray with power—but how?

This classic volume, *Quiet Talks on Prayer*, identifies prayer as the world's greatest "outlet of power," encouraging a vibrant, two-way communication with the God who longs for communion with His people. It explains the meaning and mission of prayer, hindrances to prayer, the "how-tos" of praying, and Jesus' habits of prayer.

Author S. D. (Samuel Dickey) Gordon was born in Philadelphia in 1859 and went on to author twenty-five books, all but three with "Quiet Talks" in the title—on service, about Jesus, on John's Gospel, on following the Christ, etc. But his *Quiet Talks on Prayer* may be his best known.

Gordon has been described as a "plain man" who earned no educational degrees beyond his public school diploma. But his own deep study of the Bible and his earnest method of communicating his findings led him to travel and speak widely, as far away as England and the continents of Europe and Asia. His "quiet talking" style contributed to the titles of his books. A leader in the Young Men's Christian

Associations of Pennsylvania and Ohio in the late nineteenth century, Gordon lived until 1936, dying at age seventy-six.

This edition of *Quiet Talks on Prayer* has been lightly updated for ease of reading. It has also been abridged, to approximately two-thirds of its original length.

I.
The Meaning and Mission of Prayer

1

Prayer:
The Greatest Outlet
of Power

Five Outlets of Power

A great sorrow has come into the heart of God. One of His worlds is a prodigal! *Ours* is that prodigal world, and we have *consented* to the prodigal part of the story. But He has won some of us back with His strong, tender love. And we won ones may be the pathway back to God for the others. That is His earnest desire. That should be our dominant ambition. For that purpose He has endowed us with unique power.

There is one inlet of power in the life—the Holy Spirit. He is power. He is in everyone who opens his door to God. He eagerly enters every open door. He comes in by our invitation and consent. His presence within is the vital thing.

But with many of us, while He is inside, He

is not in control. He is inside as guest, not as host. He is hindered in His natural movements so that He cannot do what He wants. And so we are not conscious or are only partially conscious of His presence. And others are still less so. But to yield to His mastery, to cultivate His friendship, to give Him full sway—that will result in what is called power.

There are five outlets of power through which this One within shows Himself and reveals His power.

First: through the life, what we are. If we are right with God, the power of God will be constantly flowing out of us, though we are not conscious of it. There will be an eager desire to serve. Yet we may constantly accomplish more in what we are than in what we do. We may serve better in the lives we live than in the best service we ever give. The memory of that should bring rest to your spirit when you are tired and disheartened because of that tiredness.

Second: through the lips, what we say. It maybe said falteringly, but if said your best with the desire to please the Master, it will be God blessed. Do your best and leave the rest. If we are in touch with God His fire burns whether the tongue stammers or has good control of its powers.

Third: through our service, what we do. Your best may not be *the* best, but if it is your best it will bring a harvest.

Fourth: through our money, what we do not keep but release for God. Money comes the nearest to omnipotence of anything we handle.

And fifth: through our prayer, what we claim in Jesus' name.

And by all odds the greatest of these is the outlet through prayer. The power of a life touches just one spot, though the touch is tremendous. What is there to be compared with a pure, unselfish, gently strong life? Yet its power is limited to one spot where it is being lived. Power through the lips depends wholly upon the life behind the lips. Power through service may be great, yet it is always less than that of a life. Power through money depends wholly upon the motive behind the money. But the power loosened through prayer is as tremendous as the power of a true fragrant life and may touch not just one spot but wherever in the whole world you may choose to turn it.

The greatest thing anyone can do for God and for man is to pray. It is not the only thing, but it is the chief thing. A correct balancing of the possible powers one may exert puts it first.

For if a man is to pray right, he must first *be* right in his motives and life. And if a man *is* right and puts the practice of praying in its rightful place, then his serving and giving and speaking will be fragrant with the presence of God.

The great people of the earth today are the people who pray. I do not mean those who talk about prayer, nor those who say they believe in prayer, nor yet those who can explain about prayer; but I mean these people who *take* time and *pray.* They do not have time. It must be taken from something else. This something else is impor-tant, and more pressing than prayer. There are people who put prayer first and group the other items in life's schedule around and after prayer.

These are the people today who are doing the most for God: in winning souls, solving problems, awakening churches, supplying people and money for mission posts, and keeping the old earth sweet awhile longer.

It is wholly a secret service. We do not know who these people are, though sometimes shrewd guesses may be made. I often think that sometimes we pass some plain-looking woman quietly slipping out of church and we hardly give her a passing thought, not knowing or guessing that perhaps *she* is the one who is doing far more for her church and the world and God than a hundred who would claim more attention and thought *because she prays* as the Spirit of God inspires and guides.

Let me put it this way: God will do as a result of the praying of the humblest one here what otherwise He *would* not do. Yes, I can put it stronger than that, for the Book does. God will do in answer to the prayer of the weakest one here what otherwise He *could* not do. Listen to Jesus' own words in that last long quiet talk He had with the eleven men between the upper room and the olive grove. "You did not choose Me, but I chose you and appointed you that you should go and bear fruit, and that your fruit should remain, that whatever you ask the Father in My name He *may* give you" (John 15:16, emphasis added). Mark that word *may*; not *shall* this time but *may*. "Shall" throws the matter over on God—His purpose. "May" throws it over on us—our cooperation. That is to say, our praying makes it possible for God to do what otherwise He could not do.

And if you think about it a bit, this fits in with the true concept of prayer. In its simplest analysis, all prayer must have two parts. First, a God to give, and second, *a man to receive.* Man's willingness is God's channel to the earth. God never crowds or coerces. Everything God does for man and through man He does with man's consent, always. Let it be said that God can do nothing for the man with shut hand and shut life. There must be an open hand and heart and life *through* which God can give what He longs to. An open life, an open hand is the pipeline of communication between the heart of God and this poor world. Our prayer is God's opportunity to get into the world that shuts Him out.

In Touch with a Planet

Prayer opens a whole planet to a man's activities. I can come as close to touching hearts for God in faraway India or China through prayer as if I were there. Not in as many ways as though there, but as truly. I think the highest possible privilege of service is in those far-off lands. There the need is greatest, the darkness densest, and the pleading call most eloquently pathetic. And if one *may* go there, if one is *privileged* to go to the honored place of service, he may then use all five outlets in the spot where he is.

Yet this is only one spot. But his relationship is as wide as his Master's and his sympathies should be. A man may be in Africa, but if his heart is in touch with Jesus it will be burning for *a world*. Prayer puts us into direct, dynamic touch with a world.

If a man may come as close to spending a half hour in India for God as if he were there in person, surely you and I must get more half hours for this secret service. Without any doubt he may be for a time truly present at the objective point of his prayer. He may give a new meaning to the printed page being read by some native down in Africa. He may give a new tongue of flame to the preacher or teacher. He may make it easier for men to accept the story of Jesus and then to yield themselves to Jesus.

You may be thinking that if you were there you could influence men by your personal contact, by the living voice. So you could. And there must be the personal touch. But no matter where you are you do more through your praying than through your personality. If you were in India you could *add your personality to your prayer*. That would be a great thing to do. But whether there or here, you must first win the victory, every step, every life, every foot of the way, in secret, in the spirit realm, and then add the mighty touch of your personality in service. You can do *more* than pray, *after* you have prayed.

But you can *not* do more than pray *until* you have prayed. And that is where we have all seemed to make a slip at times. We think we can do more where we are through our service than prayer to give power to service. *No*, we can do nothing of real power until we have done the prayer thing.

Here is a man by my side. I can talk to him. I can bring my personality to bear upon him, that I may win him. But before I can influence his will at all for God, I must first have won the victory in the secret place. Intercession is winning the victory over the chief, and service is taking the field after the chief is driven off. Such service is limited by the limitation of personality to one place.

Some of our more practical friends may say, "Prayer is good and right, but the great need is to be doing something practical." The truth is that when one puts prayer in its right place in his life, he finds a new motivating power burning in his bones to be *doing*; and furthermore, he finds that the doing that grows out of praying is mightiest in touching human hearts. And he finds further with great joy that he may be *doing* something for an entire world. His service becomes as broad as his Master's thought.

Intercession Is Service

Intercession is service: the chief service of a life according to God's plan. It is unlike all other forms of service and superior to them in this: it has fewer limitations. In all other service we are constantly limited by space, bodily strength, equipment, material obstacles, and difficulties involved with differences of personality. Prayer knows no such limitations. It goes directly into men's hearts, quietly passes through walls, and comes into most direct touch with the inner heart and will.

The whole circle of endeavor in winning people includes an infinite variety. There is speaking the truth to a number of persons, as well as to one at a time; the doing of kindly acts of helpfulness; teaching; the almost omnipotent ministry of money; letter writing; printer's ink in endless variety. All these are in God's plan for winning men. But the intensely fascinating fact to mark is this: the real victory in all of this service is won in secret, beforehand, by prayer, and these other indispensable things are the moving on the works of the enemy and claiming the victory already won. Then we go into service with a spirit of expectancy that sweeps the field at the start and steadily persists on the stubbornly contested spots until the whipped foe turns tail and runs. Prayer is striking the winning blow at the concealed enemy. Service is gathering up the results of that blow among the people we see and touch. Great patience and tact and persistence are needed in service because each person must be influenced in his own will. But the shrewd strategy that wins puts the secret fighting first.

The Broad Inner Horizon

The rightly rounded Christian life has two sides: the *out*side and the *inner* side. To most of us the outer side seems the greater. The living, the serving, the giving, the doing, the absorption in life's work, the contact with people—these take the greater thought and time of us all. They seem to be the great business of life even to those of us who thoroughly believe in the inner life.

But when the inner eyes open, the change of perspective is first ludicrous, then terrific, then pathetic. Ludicrous, because of the change of proportions; terrific, because of the issues at stake; pathetic, because of strong men that see not and keep spending their strength whittling sticks. The outer side is narrow in its limits. It has to do with food and clothing, bricks and lumber, time and the passing hour, the culture of the mind, the joys of social contact, the smoothing of the way for the suffering. And it needs not be said that these are right; they belong in the picture; they are its physical background.

The inner side *includes all of these*, and stretches infinitely beyond. Its limits are broad. It touches the inner spirit. It moves in upon the motives, the loves, the heart. It moves out upon the myriad spirit beings. It moves up to the arm of God in cooperation with His great love-plan for a world.

Shall we follow for a day one who has gotten the true perspective? Here is the outer side: a humble home, checking a ledger, pushing the plow, tending the stock, doing the chores, and all the rest of the endless, day-by-day, commonplace duties that must be done. This one whom we are following unseen is quietly, cheerfully doing his daily round, with a bit of sunshine in his face, a light in his eye, and lightness in his step, and the commonplace becomes uncommon because of the presence of this man with the uncommon spirit. He is working for God. No, better, he is working with God. He has an unseen Friend at his side. That changes all. The common drudgery ceases to be common and ceases to be drudgery because it is done for such an uncommon Master.

Now here is the inner side where the larger work of life is being done. Here is the quiet bit of time alone with God, with the Book. The door is shut, as the Master said. Now it is the morning hour with a bit of artificial light, for the sun is busy yet farther east. Now it is the evening hour, with the sun speeding toward western service, and the bed invitingly near. There is a looking up into God's face then reverent reading, and then a simple, intelligent pleading with its many variations of this—"Your will be done, in the Victor's name." God Himself is here, in this inner room. The angels are here. This room opens out into and is in direct touch with a spirit space as wide as the earth. The horizon of this room is as broad as the globe. God's presence with this man makes it so.

Today a half hour is spent in China, for its missionaries, its native Christians, its millions. And in through the petitions runs this golden thread—"Victory in Jesus' name today. Your will be done." Tomorrow's bit of time is largely spent in India perhaps. And so this man with the narrow outer horizon and the broad inner horizon pushes his spirit way around the world. The tide of prayer sweeps quietly, relentlessly day by day.

This is the true Christian life. This man is winning souls and refreshing lives in these far-off lands and in nearby places as truly as though he were in each place. This is the Master's plan. The true follower of Jesus has as broad a horizon as his Master. Jesus thought in continents and seas. His follower prays in continents and seas.

There comes to this man occasional evidences of changes being wrought, yet he knows that these are but the thin line of glory light that speaks of the fuller shining. And with a spirit touched with glad awe that he can help God, a heart full of peace and yearning, and a life fragrant with an unseen Presence he goes steadily on his way.

2

❖

Prayer:
The Deciding Factor
in a Spirit Conflict

A Prehistoric Conflict

In its simplest meaning, prayer has to do with a conflict. It is the deciding factor in a spirit conflict. The scene of the conflict is the earth. The purpose of the conflict is to decide the control of the earth and its inhabitants. The conflict runs back into the misty ages of the creation time.

The rightful Prince of the earth is Jesus, the King's Son. There is a pretender prince who was once rightful prince. He was guilty of a breach of trust. But like King Saul, after his rejection and David's anointing in his place, he has been and is trying his best to hold the realm and oust the rightful ruler.

The rightful Prince is seeking by utterly different means—namely, persuasion—to win the world back to its first allegiance. He had a fierce run-in with the pretender, and after a series of victories won the great victory of the resurrection morning.

There is one peculiarity of this conflict that makes it different from all others: a decided victory and the utter vanquishing of the leading general has not stopped the war. And the reason is remarkable. The Victor has a deep love-ambition to not merely beat the enemy but *win men's hearts, by their free consent.* And so, with marvelous love born of wisdom and courage, the conflict is left open, for men's sake.

It is a spirit conflict. There are unnumbered thousands of spirit beings good and evil, tramping the earth's surface and filling its atmosphere. They are organized into two compact organizations.

Man is an embodied spirit being. He has a body and a mind. He is a spirit. His real conflicts are of the spirit sort, in the spirit realm, with other spirit beings.

Satan is an unembodied spirit being, unembodied, that is, except when with much cunning and dark purpose he secures embodiment in human beings.

The only sort of power that influences in the spirit realm is *moral* power. By this I do not mean *goodness*, but that sort of power, either bad or good, that is infinitely higher and greater than the mere physical. Moral power is the opposite of violent or physical power.

God does not use force. There are some exceptions to this statement. In extreme instances God has ordered war measures. The nations that Israel was told to remove by the death of war would have inevitably worn themselves out through their physical excesses and disobedience of the laws of life. But a wide view of the race revealed an emergency that demanded a speedier movement. And as an exception, for the sake of His plan for the ultimate saving of a race, and a world, God gave an extermination order. The emergency makes the exception. There is one circumstance under which the taking of human life is right, namely, when it can be clearly established that God the giver and sovereign of life has so directed. But the rule is clearly that God does not use force.

But in sharp contrast, physical force is one of Satan's chief weapons. But there are two interesting facts: first, he can use it only as he secures man as his ally and uses it through him. And, second, in using it he has with great subtlety sought to shift the sphere of action.

He knows that in the sphere of spirit force he is defeated. For there is a moral force on the other side greater than any at his command. The forces of purity and righteousness he simply *cannot* withstand. Jesus is the personification of purity and righteousness. It was in this spirit sphere that He won the great victory with His purity and righteousness unstained.

Prayer Is Projecting One's Spirit Personality

Now prayer is a spirit force; it has to do wholly with spirit beings and forces. It is an insistent claiming by a man that the power of Jesus' victory over the great evil-spirit chieftain will extend to particular lives now under his control. The prayer takes on the characteristic of the man praying. He is a spirit being. It becomes a spirit force. It is a projecting into the spirit realm of his spirit personality. Being a spirit force, it has certain qualities or characteristics of disembodied spirit beings. A disembodied spirit being is not limited by space as we embodied folk are. It can go as swiftly as we can think.

Further, spirit beings are not limited by material obstructions such as the walls of buildings. Prayer is really projecting my spirit, that is, my real personality, to the spot concerned and doing business there with other spirit beings. For example, there is a man in a city on the Atlantic Seaboard for whom I pray daily. It makes my praying for him tangible and definite to recall that every time I pray my prayer is a spirit force instantly traversing the space between him and me and influencing the spirit beings surrounding him, and so influencing his own will.

When it became clear to me some few years ago that my Master would not have me go to those parts of the earth where the need is greatest, a deep tinge of disappointment came over me. Then as I realized the wisdom of His sovereignty in service, it came to me anew that I could exert a positive influence in those lands for Him by prayer. As many others have done, I marked out a daily schedule of prayer. There are certain ones for whom I pray by name, at certain intervals. And it gives great simplicity to my faith and great gladness to my heart to remember that every time such prayer is breathed out, my spirit personality is being projected yonder, and in effect I am standing in Shanghai and Calcutta and Tokyo in turn and pleading the power of Jesus' victory over the evil one there, and on behalf of those faithful ones standing there for God.

It is a fiercely contested conflict. Satan is a

trained strategist and an obstinate fighter. He refuses to acknowledge defeat until he must. It is the fight of his life. Prayer is insisting on Jesus' victory and on the retreat of the enemy on each particular spot and heart and problem concerned.

The enemy yields only what he must. He yields only what is taken, therefore the ground must be taken step by step. Prayer must be definite. He yields only when he must, therefore the prayer must be persistent. He continually renews his attacks, therefore the ground taken must be *held* against him in the Victor's name. This helps to understand why prayer must be persisted in after we have full assurance of the result, and even after some immediate results have come, or after the general results have started coming.

Giving God a Fresh Footing

The Victor's best ally in this conflict is the man, who while he remains down on the battlefield, puts his life in full touch with his Savior-Victor and then incessantly claims *victory in Jesus' name*. He is the one foe among men whom Satan cannot withstand. He is projecting an irresistible spirit force into the spirit realm. Satan is obliged to yield.

If we had eyes to see spirit beings and spirit conflicts, we would constantly see the enemy's defeat in numberless instances through the persistent praying of someone allied to Jesus in the spirit of his life. Every time such a person prays it is a waving of the red flag of Jesus Christ above Satan's head in the spirit world. Everyone who freely gives themselves over to God and gives themselves up to prayer is giving God a new spot in the contested territory on which to erect His banner of victory.

Prayer is a person giving God a footing on the contested territory of this earth. The person in full touch with God, insistently praying, is God's footing on the enemy's soil. The person wholly given over to God gives Him a new sub-headquarters on the battlefield from which to work. And the Holy Spirit within that person, on the new spot, will insist on the enemy's retreat in Jesus the Victor's name. That is prayer.

3

❖

Earth:
The Battlefield in Prayer

Prayer, a War Measure

The heart of God bleeds over the world, His
prodigal son. It has been gone so long, and the
home circle is broken. He has spent all the wealth
of His thought on a plan for winning the prodigal
back home. Angels and men have marveled over
that plan. He needs man for His plan. He will
use man. He will *honor* man in service. But these
only touch the edge of the truth. The pathway
from God to a human heart is through a human
heart. When He came to the great strategic move
in His plan, He Himself came down as a man
and made that move. *He needs man for His plan.*

The greatest agency put into man's hands is
prayer. To understand that fully one needs to
define prayer. And to define prayer adequately
one must use the language of war. Peace language

is not equal to the situation. The earth is in a state of war. It is being hotly besieged, so one must use war talk to grasp the facts with which prayer is concerned. *Prayer from God's side is communication between Himself and His allies in the enemy's country.* Prayer is not persuading God. It does not influence God's purpose. He is far more eager for what we are rightly eager for than we ever are. What there is of wrong and sin and suffering that pains you pains Him far more. He is more keenly sensitive to it than the most sensitive one of us. Whatever of heart yearning there may be that moves you to prayer is from Him. God takes the initiative in all prayer. It starts with Him.

Three Forms of Prayer

Prayer is the word commonly used for all communication with God. But it should be kept in mind that that word covers and includes three forms of communication. All prayer grows up through and ever continues in three stages.

The first form of prayer is *communion.* That is simply being on good terms with God. It involves the blood of the cross as the basis of our getting and being on good terms. It involves my coming to God through Jesus. It is fellowship with God.

Not asking for some particular thing but simply enjoying Him, loving Him, thinking about Him, talking to Him without words. That is the truest worship, thinking how worthy He is of all the best we can possibly bring to Him, and infinitely more. Of necessity it includes confession on my part and forgiveness on God's part, for only with those can we come into the relation of fellowship. Adoration and worship belong to this first phase of prayer.

The second form of prayer is *petition*. And I am using that word now in the narrower meaning of asking something for one's self. Petition is a definite request of God for something I need. A man's whole life is utterly dependent upon the giving hand of God. Everything we need comes from Him. There needs to be a constant stream of petition going up, many times wordless prayer. And there will be a constant return stream of answer and supply coming down. The door between God and one's own self must be kept ever open. The knob to be turned is on our side. He opened His side long ago, propped it open, and threw the knob away. The whole life hinges upon this continual communication with our wondrous God.

The third form of prayer is *intercession*. True

prayer never stops with petition for one's self. It reaches out for others. The very word *intercession* implies a reaching out for someone else. It is standing as a go-between, a mutual friend, between God and someone who is either out of touch with Him or is needing special help. Intercession is the climax of prayer. It is the outward drive of prayer. It is the effective end of prayer *outward*. Communion and petition are upward and downward. Intercession rests upon these two as its foundation. Communion and petition store the life with the power of God; intercession lets it out on behalf of others. The first two are necessary for self and ally a man fully with God; this third makes use of that alliance for others. Intercession is the form of prayer that helps God in His great love-plan for winning a planet back to its true sphere.

The Climax of Prayer

To God, man is first an objective point, and then he further becomes a distributing center. God ever thinks of a man doubly: first for his own self, and then for his possible use in reaching others. Communion and petition fix and continue one's relationship to God and so prepare for the great outreaching form of prayer—intercession. Prayer must begin in the first two but reaches its climax in the third. Communion and petition are of necessity self-wide. Intercession is worldwide in its reach. And all true rounded prayer will ever have all three elements in it.

Six Facts Underlying Prayer

There are certain facts constantly stated and assumed in the old Book. They are clearly stated in its history, they are woven into its songs, and they underlie all the prophetic writings. Here is a chain of six facts:

First: "The earth is the LORD's, and all its fullness" (Psalm 24:1). His by creation and by sovereign rule. "The LORD sat enthroned at the Flood" (Psalm 29:10).

Second: God gave the dominion of the earth to man: the kingship of its life and the control and mastery of its forces. (See Genesis 1:26, 28; Psalm 8:6.)

Third: man transferred his dominion to somebody else, by a double act. He was deceived into doing that act, one of disobedience and of obedience: disobedience to God and obedience to another one, a prince who was seeking to get the dominion of the earth into his own hands. That act of the first man did this. The disobedience transferred his allegiance from God. The obedience to the other one transferred the allegiance and, through that, the dominion to the other one.

Fourth: the dominion of this earth, as far as was given to man, is not God's, for He gave it to man. And it is not man's, for he has transferred it to another. It is in the control of that prince whose changed character supplies his name— Satan, the hater, the enemy. Jesus repeatedly spoke of "the ruler of this world." (See John 12:31; 14:30; 16:11.) John spoke in Revelation of a time coming when "the kingdoms of this world [will] have become the kingdoms of our Lord and of His Christ!" (Revelation 11:15). By clear inference previous to that time it is somebody's kingdom other than His. The kingship of the earth that was given to man is now Satan's.

Fifth: God was eager to swing the world back to its original sway: for His own sake, for man's sake, for the earth's sake. You see, we do not know God's world as it came from His hand. It is an exquisitely beautiful world even yet, but it is not the world it was, nor what someday it will be. It has been sadly scarred and changed under its present ruler.

God was eager to swing the old world back

to its original control. But to do so He must get a man, one of the original trustee class through whom He might swing it back to its first allegiance. It was given to man. It was swung away by man. It must be swung back by man. And so a Man came, and while Jesus was perfectly and utterly human, we spell that word *Man* with a capital *M* because He was a man quite distinct from all men. Because He was more truly human than all other men, He is quite apart from other men. This Man was to head a movement for swinging the world back to its first allegiance.

Sixth: God's Man and the pretender-prince had a combat: the most terrific combat ever waged or witnessed. From the cruel, malicious cradle attack until Calvary's morning and two days longer it ran. Through those thirty-three years it continued with an intensity unknown before or since. The master-prince of subtlety and force did his best and his worst through those Nazareth years, then into the wilderness, Gethsemane, and Calvary. That day at three o'clock and for a bit longer the evil one thought he had won, and there was great glee in the headquarters of the prince of this world. They thought the victory was theirs when God's Man lay in the grave under the bars of death, within the immediate control of the lord of death. But the third morning came and the bars of death were snapped like thread. *Jesus rose a Victor.* For it was not possible that such as *He* could be held by death's lord. And then Satan knew that he was defeated. Jesus, God's Man, the King's rightful Prince, had gotten the victory.

But mark carefully four subfacts on Satan's side. First, he refuses to acknowledge his defeat. Second, he refuses to surrender his dominion until he must. He yields only what he must and when he must. Third, he is supported in his ambitions by man. He has man's consent to his control. The majority of men on the earth today have assented to his control. (Satan *cannot* get into a man's heart without his consent, and God *will* not.) And fourth, he still hopes to make his possession of the earth permanent.

The Victor's Great Plan
Now, note on the side of the Victor-Prince this unparalleled action: He has left the conflict open and the defeated chief on the field that He may not simply beat the chief but through that victory win the whole prodigal race back to His Father's home circle. But the great battle is yet to come. Jesus rides into the future fight a

Victor. Satan will fight his last fight under the shadow and sting of a defeat. He is apparently trying hard to get at Jesus. That is to say, Jesus was God's Man sent down to swing the world back. Satan is trying his best to get *a man* who will stand for him even as Jesus stood for God, a man who will personify himself even as Jesus was the personification of God. When he succeeds in that, the last desperate crisis will come.

Now prayer is this: a person with his life in full touch with the Victor and out of touch with the pretender-prince, insistently claiming that Satan will yield before Jesus' victory, step by step, life after life. Jesus is the Victor. Satan knows it, and fears Him. He must yield before His advance, and he must yield before this person who stands for Jesus on the earth. And he *will* yield. Reluctantly, angrily, stubbornly contesting every inch of ground, his clutches will loosen and he will go before this Jesus-man.

Jesus said, "The ruler of this world is coming, and he has nothing in Me" (John 14:30). When you and I, resolute, humbly depending on His grace, say, "Though the prince of this world comes, he will have nothing in me," then we will be in the position where Satan must yield as we claim victory in the Victor's name.

4

❖

DOES PRAYER INFLUENCE GOD?

How God Gives

Someone may object that God's Word does not agree with this point of view.

My memory brings up a few familiar passages. "Call to Me, and I will answer you, and show you great and mighty things, which you do not know" (Jeremiah 33:3). "Call upon Me in the day of trouble; I will deliver you, and you shall glorify Me" (Psalm 50:15). "Ask, and it will be given to you; seek, and you will find; knock, and it will be opened to you" (Matthew 7:7). We have for generations been accustomed to think that our asking is the thing that influences God and, further, that many times persistent, continued asking is necessary to induce God to do something. The usual explanation for this need of persistence is that God is testing our faith and seeking to make certain changes in us before granting our requests. This explanation is without doubt quite true, *in part*.

We seem to learn about God best by analogies. The analogy never brings all there is to be learned, yet it seems to be the nearest we can get. From what we know of ourselves we come to know Him.

Among those who give to benevolent enter-prises there are three sorts of givers, with varia-tions in each. There is the man who gives because he is influenced by others. If the right man or committee of men calls and skillfully presents their pleas, he eventually gives. At first he seems reluctant but finally gives with more or less grace.

There is a second sort: the man of truly bene-volent heart who is desirous of giving that he may be of help to others. He listens attentively when pleas come to him and waits only long enough to satisfy himself of the worth of the cause and the proper amount to give, and then gives.

The third sort is the rarest: the man who *takes the initiative*. He looks about him, makes inquiries, and thinks over the great need of his fellow man in every direction. He decides where his money may best be used to help and then offers to give. But his gift may be abused by some who would get at his money if they could and use it unwisely or otherwise than he intends. So he makes certain conditions that must be met.

Any human illustration of God must seem crude. Yet of these three sorts of givers there is only one that begins to suggest how God gives. It may seem like a sweeping statement to make, yet I am more and more disposed to believe it true that *most people* have unknowingly thought of God's answering prayer as the first of these three people give. Many others have had in mind some such thought as the second suggests, yet neither of these ways in any manner illustrates God's giving. The third comes the nearest to picturing the God who hears and answers prayer. Our God has a great heart yearning after His poor prodigal world and each one in it. He longs to have the effects of sin removed and the original image restored. He takes the initiative. Yet everything that is done for man must of necessity be through man's will. The obstacles are not numberless nor insurmountable, but they are many and they are stubborn. There is a cunning pretender-prince who is a past-master in the fine art of handling men. There are wills warped and weakened, consciences blurred, sensibilities whose edge has been dulled. Sin has not only stained the life but warped the judgment, sapped the will, and blurred the mental vision. And God has a hard time just because every change must be through that sapped and warped will.

Yet the difficulty is never complex but very simple. And so the statement of His purpose is ever exquisitely simple. "Call to Me, and I will answer you, and show you great and mighty things, which you do not know" (Jeremiah 33:3). If a man calls, he has already turned his face toward God. His will has acted, and acted doubly: away from the opposite and *toward* God. The calling is the point of sympathetic contact with God where their purposes become the same. The caller is beset by difficulties and longs for freedom. The God who speaks to him saw the difficulties long ago and eagerly longed to remove them. Now they have come to agreement. And through this willing will God eagerly works out His purpose.

A Very Old Question

This leads to a very old question: Does prayer influence God? No question has been discussed more, or more earnestly. Skeptical men of fine scientific training have with great certainty said no. And Christian men of scholarly training and strong faith have with equal certainty said yes. Strange to say, both have been right. Not right in all their statements, nor right in all their beliefs, nor right in all their processes of thinking, but right in their ultimate conclusions as represented by the short words *no* and *yes*. Prayer does not influence God. Prayer surely does influence God. It does not influence His purpose. It does influence His action. Every right thing that has ever been prayed for God has already purposed to do. But He does nothing without our consent. He has been hindered in His purposes by our lack of willingness. When we learn His purposes and make them our prayers, we are giving Him the opportunity to act. It is a double opportunity: manward and Satanward. We are willing. Our willingness checkmates Satan's opposition. It opens the path to God and rids it of the obstacles, and so the road is cleared for the free action already planned.

Emergencies change all habits of action, divine and human. They are the real test of power. *The world is in a great emergency through sin.* Only as that tremendous fact grips us will we be people of prayer and people of action up to the limit of the need and to the limit of the possibilities.

Only as that intense fact is kept in mind will we begin to understand God's actions in history and in our personal experiences. The greatest event of earth, the cross, was an emergency action.

The fact that prayer does not make any change in God's thought or purpose reveals His marvelous love in a very tender way.

Suppose I want and *need* something very much, and I go to God and ask for it. And suppose He is reluctant about giving it. But I am insistent, and plead and persist, and by and by God is impressed with my earnestness and sees that I really need the thing, answers my prayer, and gives me what I ask. Is not that a loving God to listen and yield to my plea? Surely.

But suppose God is thinking about me all the time and lovingly planning for me and longing to give me much that He has. Yet in His wisdom He does not give because I do not know my own need and have not opened my hand to receive, and, further, not knowing my need, I might abuse, misuse, or fail to use something given before I felt the need of it. And now I see and feel that need and come and ask and He, delighted with the change in me, eagerly gives. Tell me, is not that a very much more loving God than the other conception suggests? The truth is, *that* is God. Jesus says, "Your Father knows the things you have need of *before you ask Him*" (Matthew 6:8, emphasis added). And He is a Father. And with God the word *father* means mother, too. Then what He *knows* we need He has *already planned* to give. The great question for me then in praying for some personal thing is this: Do *I* know what *He* knows I need? Am I thinking about what He is thinking about for me?

And then remember that God is so much better in His loving planning than the wisest, most loving father we know. Does a mother think about her child's needs, the food and clothing and luxuries? That is God, only He is more loving and wiser than the best of us. He is thinking about me. He knows what I am thinking of and what I would most enjoy, and He is such a lover-God that He would choose something just a bit finer than I would think. Prayer does not and cannot change the purpose of such a God. For every right and good thing we might ask for He has already planned to give us. But prayer does change the action of God because He cannot give against our wills, and our willingness as expressed by our asking gives Him the opportunity to do as He has already planned.

The Greatest Prayer

There is a greatest prayer that can be offered. It is the undercurrent in the stream of all Spirit-breathed prayer. Jesus Himself gives it to us in the only form of prayer He left for our use. It is small in size but mighty in power. Four words: "Your will be done." Let us meditate on it, that its fragrance may come up into our nostrils and fill our very beings.

"Your": That is God. On one side, He is wise. On another side, He is strong. On still another side He is good, pure, and holy. Then on a side remaining, the tender personal side, He is— loving? No, that is quite inadequate. He is *love*. He personifies love. Now remember that love means infinitely more than we think. Its meaning is measurelessly beyond our highest reach.

And then, this God, wise, strong, good, and love, *is related to us*. We belong to Him. We are His children by creation, and by a new creation in Jesus Christ. He is ours, by His own act. That is the "Your"—a God who is a father-mother-God, and is *our* God.

"Your *will*." God's will is His desires, His purposes, that which He wishes to occur, and that to which He gives His strength that it may occur. The earth is His creation. Men are

His children. He has given Himself to thinking and studying and planning for all men and for the earth. His plan is the most wise, pure, loving plan that can be thought of, *and more*. Nothing escapes the love-vigilance of our God. Health, strength, home, loved ones, friendships, money, guidance, protecting care, the necessities, the extras that love ever thinks of, service—all these are included in God's loving thought for us. That is His will. It is modified by the degree of our consent, and further modified by the circumstances of our lives. Life has become a badly tangled skein of threads. With infinite patience and skill God is at work untangling and bringing the best possible out of the tangle. What is absolutely best is rarely relatively best. That which is best in itself is usually not best under certain circumstances, with human lives in the balance. God has fathomless skill, measureless patience, and a love utterly beyond both. He is ever working out the best thing possible under every circumstance. He could often do more, and do it in much less time if our human wills were more compliant with His.

He can be trusted in the darkest dark where you cannot see. And trust does not mean test. Where you trust you do not test. Where you test you do not trust. Making this our prayer means trusting God. A man's will is the man in action, within the limits of his power. God's will for man is Himself in action, within the limits of our cooperation. The greatest strength is revealed in intelligent yielding. Here the prayer is expressing the utter willingness of a man that God's will be done in him and through him. Here he makes his will as strong as it can be made, like the strong oak, strong enough to sway and bend in the wind. Then he uses all its strength in becoming passive to a higher will, even when the purpose of that higher will is not clear to his own limited knowledge and understanding.

"Your will be *done*." That is, be accomplished. The word stands for the action in its perfected, finished state. It speaks not only of the earnest desire of the heart praying but the set purpose that everything in the life be held subject to the doing of this purpose of God. It means that surrender of purpose that has utterly changed the lives of the strongest men in order that the purpose of God might be dominant. It cut off from a great throne earth's greatest jurist, the Hebrew lawgiver, and led him instead to be allied to a race of slaves. It led that intellectual giant Jeremiah from an easy, enjoyable leadership to espouse a despised cause and so be himself despised. It led Paul from the leadership of his generation in a great nation to untold suffering, and to a block and an ax. It led Jesus, the very Son of God, away from a kingship to a cross. In every generation it has radically changed lives, and life ambitions. "Your will be done" is the great dominant purpose-prayer that has been the pathway of God in all His great doings among men.

With this prayer go two clauses that explain it. They are included in it and are added to make more clear the full intent. The first of these clauses gives the sweep of His will in its broadest outlines. The second touches the opposition to that will for our individual lives, the human race, and the earth.

The first clause is this: "Your kingdom come." In both of these short sentences—"Your will be done," "Your kingdom come"—the emphatic word is "Your." That word is set in sharpest possible contrast here. There is another kingdom now on the earth. There is another will being done. This other kingdom must go if God's kingdom is to come. These kingdoms are antagonistic at every point of contact. They are rivals for the same allegiance and the same territory. They cannot exist together.

The second clause included in the prayer is this: "Deliver us from the evil one." These two sentences—"Your will be done" and "deliver us from the evil one"—are naturally connected. Each statement includes the other. To have God's will fully done in us means emancipation from every influence of the evil one. To be delivered from the evil one means that every thought and plan of God for our lives will be fully carried out.

The two great wills at work in the world are ever clashing in the action of history and in our individual lives. In all of us, in varying degrees, these two wills constantly clash. Man is the real battlefield. The pitch of the battle is in his will. God will not do His will in a man without the man's will consenting. And Satan cannot. The one thing that works against God's will is the evil one's will. On the other hand, the one thing that effectively thwarts Satan's plans is a man wholly given up to God's will.

The greatest prayer then fully expressed sweeps first the whole field of action, then touches the heart of the action, and then attacks the opposition. It is this: "Your kingdom come: Your will be done; deliver us from the evil one." Every true prayer ever offered comes under this simple, comprehensive prayer. It includes all other petitions, for God's will includes everything for which prayer is rightly offered. It hits the very bull's-eye of opposition to God.

II.
Hindrances
to Prayer

1

Why the Results Fail

Breaking with God

God answers prayer. Prayer is God and man joining hands to secure some high end. He joins with us through the communication of prayer in accomplishing certain great results. This is the main drive of prayer. Our asking and expecting and God's doing jointly bring to pass things that otherwise would not come to pass.

Yet a great many prayers are not answered. Probably it is accurate to say that *thousands* of prayers go up and bring nothing down. As a result many people are saying: "Well, prayer is not what you claim it is; we prayed and no answer came. Nothing was changed." And they are quite right. The problem is that what they say is not all there is to be said. There is yet more to be said that is right, too, and that changes the final conclusion radically. Partial truth is a very mean sort of lie.

The prayer plan has been much disturbed, and often broken. One who would be a partner with God up to the limit of his power must understand the things that hinder the prayer plan. There are three sorts of hindrances to prayer. First of all, there are things in us that *break off connection* with God, the source of the changing power. Then there are certain things in us that *delay* or *diminish* the results. And then there is a great *outside* hindrance to be reckoned upon. Let's discuss the first of these: the hindrances that *break off connections* between God and His human partner.

Here again there is a division into three. There are three things directly spoken of in the Bible that hinder prayer. The first one is *sin*. In Isaiah's first chapter God Himself says, "When you spread out your hands, I will hide My eyes from you; even though you make many prayers, I will not hear" (Isaiah 1:15). Why? What's the difficulty? These outstretched hands are *soiled*! They are actually holding their sin-soiled hands up into God's face, and He is compelled to look at the thing most hateful to Him. In the fifty-ninth chapter of this same book, God Himself is talking again. "Behold, the LORD's hand is not shortened. . .nor *His* ear heavy." There is no trouble on the *up* side. God is all right. "But your *iniquities*. . .your *sins*. . . your *hands*. . .your *fingers*. . .your *lips*. . .your *tongue*. . ." (Isaiah 59:1–3, emphasis added). The slime of sin is oozing over everything! Look at the sixty-sixth Psalm: "If I regard iniquity in my heart, the Lord will not hear" (66:18). How much more if the sin of the heart gets into the hands or the life! *Sin hinders prayer*. There is nothing surprising about this. That we can think the reverse is the surprising thing. Prayer is transacting business with God. Sin is *breaking with God*.

"Well," someone will object, "now you're cutting us all out, aren't you? Are we not all conscious of a sinful something inside that has to be fought all the time?" It certainly seems to be true that the nearer a man gets to God, the more keenly conscious he is of a sinful tendency even while having continual victory. But plainly what the Book means here is this: if I am holding something in my life that the Master does not like, if I am failing to obey when His voice has spoken, that to me is sin. It may be wrong in itself. It may *not* be wrong in itself. It may not be wrong for another. Sometimes it is not the thing involved but the one involved that makes the issue. If that faithful, quiet, inner voice has spoken and I know what the Master would prefer and I fail to keep in line, that to me is sin. Then prayer is a sheer waste of breath. Worse, it is deceptive. For I am apt to say or think, "Well, I am not as good as you or you, but then I am not so bad; *I pray*." The truth is, because I have broken with God, the praying is utterly worthless.

You see, *sin is slapping God in the face*. It may be polished, cultured sin, or it may be the common gutter stuff. A man is not concerned about the grain of a club that strikes him a blow. How can He and I talk together if I have done something wrong and stick to it—haven't even apologized? And of what good is an apology if the offense is being repeated? And if we cannot talk together, of course working together is out of the question. And prayer is working together with God.

Should we not throw out the thing that is wrong or put in the thing the Master wants in? For *Jesus'* sake? Indeed, for *people's* sake: poor befooled people who are being kept away because God cannot get at them through us!

Shall we bow and ask forgiveness for our sin and petty stubbornness that have been thwarting the Master's love-plan? And yet even while we ask forgiveness there are lives out there warped and dwarfed and worse because of the hindrance in us.

A Coaling Station for Satan's Fleet

There is a second thing that hinders prayer. James speaks of it in his letter. "You do not have because you do not *ask*" (James 4:2, emphasis added). That explains many parched lives and churches and unsolved problems: no pipelines run up to tap the reservoir and give God an opening into the troubled territory. Then he pushes on to say, "You ask *and do not receive*" (4:3, emphasis added). Ah! there's the rub; it is evidently an old story, this thing of not receiving. Why? "Because you ask amiss, that you may spend it *on your pleasures*" (James 4:3, emphasis added). It is self-ish praying, asking for something just because I want it for myself.

Here is a mother praying for her boy. He is growing up toward young manhood, not a Christian boy yet but a good boy. She is thinking, *I want my boy to be an honor to me; he bears my name; my blood is in his veins. I don't want my boy to be a prodigal. I want him to be a fine man, an honor to the family; and if he is a true Christian, he likely will be. I wish he were a Christian.* And so she prays and prays fervently. God might touch her boy's heart and say, "I want you out here in India to help win My prodigal world back." Oh! she did not mean that! *Her* boy in far-off India? Oh no! Not that! Yes, what *she* wanted—that was the whole thought—selfishness; no thought of sympathy with God in His eager outreach for His poor sin-befooled world. The prayer itself in its object is perfectly proper and rightly offered and answered times without number; but the *motive* is wholly selfish and the selfishness itself becomes a foothold for Satan and so the purpose of the prayer is thwarted.

Please notice that the reason prayers are not answered is not an arbitrary reluctance on God's part to do a desirable thing. He never fails to work whenever He has half a chance to work, even through men of faulty conceptions and mixed motives. The reason lies much deeper. It is this: selfishness gives Satan a footing. It gives a coaling station for his fleet on the shore of your life. And of course he does his best to prevent the prayer, or when he cannot wholly prevent, to spoil the results as far as he can.

Prayer may be properly offered for many wholly personal things: physical strength, healing, dearly loved ones, money, things that may not be necessary but only desirable and enjoyable, for ours is a loving God who would have His dear ones enjoy to the full their lives down here. But the *motive* determines the propriety of such requests. Where the whole purpose of one's life is *for Him* these things may be asked for freely as His gracious Spirit within guides. And there need be no bondage of morbid introspection. *He knows if the purpose of the heart is to please Him.*

The Shortest Way to God

A third thing spoken of as hindering prayer is an unforgiving spirit. You have noticed that Jesus speaks much about prayer and also speaks much about forgiveness. But have you noticed how over and over again He *couples* these two—prayer *and* forgiveness?

Run through the book of Matthew a moment. In the fifth chapter we read, "If you bring your gift to the altar"—that is what we call prayer—"and there remember that your brother has something *against you,* leave your gift there before the altar, and go your way. *First* be reconciled. . ." (Matthew 5:23–24, emphasis added). Here comes a man with a lamb to offer. He approaches the altar of God reverently. But as he is coming, there flashes across his mind the face of a man with whom he has had difficulty. And instantly he can feel his grip tightening on the offering and his jaw clenching at the memory. Jesus says, "If that be so, lay your lamb right down." What? Go abruptly away? Why, how the folks around the temple will talk! The shortest way to God for that man is not the way to the altar but around by that man's house. "*First* be reconciled"—keep your perspective straight, follow the right order—"*then* come and offer your gift."

In the sixth chapter He gives the form of prayer that we commonly call the Lord's Prayer. It contains seven petitions. At the close He stops to emphasize just one of the seven, the one about forgiveness. In the eighteenth chapter Jesus is talking alone with the disciples about prayer. Peter seems to remember the previous remarks about forgiveness in connection with prayer, and he asks a question. He says, "Master, how many times *must* I forgive a man? *Seven* times?" Apparently Peter thinks he is growing in grace. He can actually *think* now of forgiving a man seven times in succession. But the Master in effect says, "Peter, you haven't caught the idea. Forgiveness is not a question of mathematics; not a matter of keeping tabs on somebody. Not seven times but *seventy times seven*." Apparently the Master is thinking that he will lose count or get tired of counting and conclude that forgiveness is preferable, or else by practice *breathe in the spirit of forgiveness*—the thing He meant.

"Well," someone says, "you do not know how hard it is to forgive." You think not? I know this much: some people and some things you *cannot* forgive by yourself. But I also know that if one allows the Spirit of Jesus to sway the heart He will make you love persons you *cannot* like. Jesus' love, when allowed to come in as freely as He means, fills your heart with pity for the person who has wounded you.

But we must forgive freely, frankly, generously if we are to be in prayer touch with God.

Since unforgiveness roots itself in hate, Satan has room for both feet in such a heart. That word *unforgiving*! What a group of relatives it has: jealousy, envy, bitterness, the cutting word, the polished shaft of sarcasm with the poisoned tip, the green eye, the acid saliva!

Search Me
Sin, selfishness, an unforgiving spirit—what searchlights these words are! God's great love-plan for His prodigal world is being held back

and lives being lost because of the lack of human prayer partners.

May we not well pray, "Search me, O God, and know my heart and help me know it. Try me and know my innermost thoughts and purposes and ambitions, and help me know them; and see what way there be in me that is a grief to You. Then lead me out of that way into *Your* way. For Jesus' sake, indeed for men's sake, too."

2

❖

WHY THE RESULTS
ARE DELAYED

God's Pathway to Human Hearts

God touches people through people. The Spirit's
path to a human heart is through another human heart. In His plan for winning men to
their true allegiance, God is limited by human
limitations. That may seem to mean more than
it really does. For our thought of the human is of
the scarred, warped, shriveled humanity that we
know, and great changes come when God's Spirit
controls. But the fact is there, however limited
our understanding of it.

God needs people for His plan. His greatest
agency for defeating the enemy and winning people back is intercession. God is counting mightily
upon that. And He can count most mightily on

the person who faithfully practices that.

The results He longs for are being held back and made smaller because so many of us have not learned how to pray simply and skillfully. We need training. And God understands that. He Himself will train. But we must be actively willing. A strong will perfectly yielded to God's will, or perfectly willing to be yielded, is His mightiest ally in redeeming the world.

Answers to prayer are delayed or denied out of kindness, *or* that more may be given, *or* that a far larger purpose may be served. But deeper down by far than that is this: *God's purposes are being delayed* because of our unwillingness to learn how to pray, *or* our slowness in learning. It is a small matter that my prayer is answered or unanswered; not small to me perhaps but small in proportion. It is a tremendous thing that *God's purpose* for a world is being held back through my lack. The thought that prayer is *getting things* from God is pitiably small and yet so common. The true conception understands that prayer is partnership with God in His planet-sized purposes.

The real reason for the delay or failure lies simply in the difference between God's viewpoint and ours. In our asking we have either not reached the *wisdom* that asks best *or* we have not reached the *unselfishness* that is willing to sacrifice a good thing for a better, or the best, the unselfishness that is willing to sacrifice the smaller personal desire for the larger thing that affects the lives of many.

We learn best by stories. This was Jesus' favorite method of teaching. In the Bible there are four striking instances of delayed answers to prayer. There are others, but these stand out sharply and perhaps include the main teachings of all. These four are Moses' request to enter Canaan; Hannah's prayer for a son; Paul's thorn; and Jesus' prayer in Gethsemane. Let us look at these in turn.

For the Sake of a Nation

First is the incident of Moses' ungranted petition. Moses is one of the giants of the human race. From his own account of his career, the secret of all his power as a maker of laws, the organizer of a strangely marvelous nation, a military general and strategist was in his direct communication with God. He was a man of prayer. Everything was referred to God, and he declared that everything— laws, organization, worship, plans—came to him from God. In national emergencies where moral catastrophe was threatened he petitioned God and the plans were changed in accordance with his request. He made personal requests and they were granted. He was a man who dealt directly with God about every sort of thing. The record commonly credited to him puts prayer as the simple, profound explanation of his stupendous career and achievements.

Now there is one exception to all this in Moses' life. It stands out the more strikingly that it is the one exception of a very long line. Moses asked repeatedly for one thing. It was not given him. God is not capricious or arbitrary. There must have been a reason. *There was*, and it is fairly luminous with light.

Here are the facts. Those freed men of Egypt were a hard lot to lead and to live with. Slow, petty, ignorant, impulsive, strangers to self-control, critical, exasperating—what an undertaking God had to make a nation, *the* nation of history, out of such stuff! What immense patience it required to shape this people. What patience God has. Moses had learned much of patience in the desert sands with his sheep, for he had learned much of God. But the finishing touches were supplied by the grindstone of friction with the fickle temper of this mob of ex-slaves.

Here are the immediate circumstances. They lacked water. They grew very thirsty. It was a serious matter in those desert sands with human lives, young children, and stock. No, it was not serious; it was really a very small matter, for *God was along* and the enterprise was of His starting. And they knew Him well enough in their brief experience to expect something fully equal to all needs with a margin thrown in.

But they forgot. Their noses were keener than their memories. They had better stomachs than hearts. The onions of Egypt made more lasting impressions than this tender, patient, planning God.

They begin to complain, to criticize. God patiently says nothing but provides for their needs. But Moses has not yet reached the high level that later experiences brought him. He is standing to them for God. Yet he is very un-Godlike. Angrily, with hot word, he *strikes* the rock. Once, striking was God's plan; then the quiet word ever after. *The waters came!* Just like God! They were cared for, though He had been disobeyed and dishonored. There were the crowds eagerly drinking with faces down, and up yonder in the shadow stands God deeply grieved at the false picture this immature people had gotten of Him that day through Moses.

Moses' hot tongue and flashing eye made a deep moral scar on their minds that would take years to remove. Something had to be done for the people's sake. Moses disobeyed and dishonored God. Yet the waters came, for *they needed water*. But they must be taught the need of obedience, the evil of disobedience, so they never could forget.

Moses was a leader. Leaders may not do as common men, and leaders may not be dealt with as followers. They affect too many lives. So God said to Moses, "You will not go into Canaan. You may lead them clear up to the line, you may even see over, but you may not go in." That hurt Moses deep down. It hurt God deeper down, in a heart more sensitive to hurt than Moses'. Without doubt it was said with reluctance, for *Moses'* sake. But it was said, plainly, irrevocably, for *their* sakes. Moses' petition was for a reversal of this decision. He wanted to see that wondrous land of God's choosing. He felt the sting, too. The edge of the knife of discipline cut keenly, and the blood spurted. But God said, "Do not speak to Me again of this." The decision was not to be changed. For Moses' sake only He would gladly have changed, judging by His previous conduct. For the sake of the nation—indeed, for the sake of the prodigal world to be won back through this nation, the petition could not be granted. That ungranted petition taught those millions the lesson of obedience, of reverence, as no command or smoking mountain or drowning Egyptians had done. It became common talk in every tent of the tented nation. With hushed tones and awed hearts the news passed from lip to lip. Some of the women and children wept. They all loved Moses. They revered him. How gladly they would have had him go over.

In later years many a Hebrew mother told her child of Moses their great leader: his appearance, his majestic mien, yet infinite tenderness and gentleness, his presence with God on the mount, the shining face. And the child would listen quietly, and then the eyes would grow big as the mother would repeat softly, "But he could not come over into the land of promise because *he did not obey God.*" And strong fathers reminded their growing sons. And so *reverent obedience to God* was woven into the warp and woof of the nation. One can well understand Moses looking down from above with grateful heart that he had been denied for *their* sakes. The unselfishness and wisdom of later years would not have made the prayer. *The prayer of a man was denied that a nation might be taught obedience.*

That More Might Be Given and Gotten

Now let us look at the portrait of Hannah the Hebrew woman. First the broader lines for perspective. The Hebrew nation had two deep dips down morally between Egypt and Babylon, between the first making and the final breaking. The national tide ebbed very low twice, before it finally ran out in the Euphrates valley. Elijah stemmed the tide the second time and saved the day for a later night. The Hannah story belongs in the first of these ebb tides, the first bad sag.

It was a leaderless people, for the true Leader as originally planned had been first ignored, then forgotten. The people had no ideals. There was a deep, hidden-away current of good, but it needed leadership to bring it to the surface. The nation was rapidly drifting down to the lowest moral level. At Shiloh the formal worship was kept up, but the priests were tainted with the worst impurity. A sort of sleepy, slovenly anarchy prevailed. Every man did what was right in his own eyes, with every indication of a gutter standard. This is the setting of the simple graphic incident of Hannah. One must get a clear mental picture to understand the story.

Up in the hill country of Ephraim there lived a wise-hearted religious man, a farmer. He was

earnest but not of the sort to rise above the habit
of his time. His farm was not far from Shiloh, the
national place of worship, and he made yearly trips
there with the family. But the woman-degrading
curse of Lamech was over his home. He had two
wives. Hannah was the loved one. (No man ever
yet gave his heart to two women.) She was a
gentle-spoken, thoughtful woman, with a deep,
earnest spirit. But she had a disappointment that
grew in intensity as it continued. The desire of
her heart had been withheld. She was childless.

Though it is not mentioned, the whole
inference is that she prayed earnestly and persistently but to her surprise and deep disappointment the desired answer came not. To
make it worse, her rival provoked and teased and
nagged her. And that went on year after year. Is
it any wonder that "she was in bitterness of soul"
and "wept in anguish" (1 Samuel 1:10)? Her
husband tenderly tried to comfort her, but her
inner spirit remained chafed to the quick. All this
went on for years, and she wondered why.

Why was it? Step back a bit and get the
broader view that the narrow limits of her
surroundings and her spirit shut out from her
eyes. Here is what she saw: her fondest hope
unrealized, long praying unanswered, a constant

ferment at home. Here is what she wanted: *a son*. That is her horizon. Beyond that her thoughts do not rise.

Here is what God saw: a nation—no, much worse—*the* nation, in which centered His great love-plan for winning His prodigal world, going to pieces. The messenger to the prodigal was being subtly seduced by the prodigal. The savior-nation was being itself lost. The plan so long and patiently fostered for saving a world was threatened with utter disaster.

Here is what He wanted: *a leader*! But there were no leaders, and there were no men out of whom leaders might be made. And worse yet, *there were no women* of the sort to train and shape a man for leadership. That is the lowest level to which a people can ever get. God had to get a woman before He could get a man. Hannah had in her the making of the woman He needed. God honored her by choosing her, but she had to be changed before she could be used. And so there came those years of pruning and sifting and discipline. And out of those years and experiences there came a new woman, a woman with vision broadened, with spirit mellowed, with strength seasoned, with will so supple as to yield to a higher will, to sacrifice the dearest *personal pleasure* for the worldwide purpose, willing that he who was her dearest treasure should be the nation's *first*.

Then followed months of prayer while the man was coming. Samuel was born, no, farther back yet, was conceived in the atmosphere of prayer and devotion to God. The prenatal influences for those months gave the sort of man God wanted. And a nation, *the* nation, the *world-plan*, was saved! This man became a living answer to prayer. The romantic story of the little boy up in the Shiloh tabernacle quickly spread over the nation. His very name—Samuel, "God hears"—sifted into people's ears the facts of a God and the power of prayer. The very sight of the boy and of the man clear to the end kept deepening the brain impression that God answers prayer. And the seeds of that rebelief in God that Samuel's leadership brought about were sown by the unusual story of his birth.

The answer was delayed that more might be given and gotten.

The Best Light for Studying a Thorn

The third great picture in this group is that of Paul and his needle-pointed thorn. First a look at Paul himself. The best light on this thorn is through the man. The man explains the thorn. What a splendid man of God he was! God's chosen one for a unique ministry. One of the twelve could be used to open the door to the great outside world, but God had to go outside this circle and get a man of different training for this wider sphere. Schooled in a Jewish atmosphere, he never lost the Jew standpoint, yet the training of his home surroundings in that outside world, the contact with Greek culture, his natural mental cast fitted him perfectly for his appointed task. His keen reasoning powers, his vivid imagination, his steel-like will, his burning devotion, his unmovable purpose, his tender attachment to his Lord— what a man! Well might the Master want to win such a man for His service.

But Paul had some weak traits. Let us just remember that where we think of one in him there come crowding to memory's door many more in one's self. A man's weak point is usually the extreme opposite swing of the pendulum on his strong point. Paul had a tremendous will. He was a Hercules in his will. Those tireless journeys with their terrific experiences all spell out *will* large and black. But he went to extremes here. Was it due to his overtired nerves? Likely enough. He was obstinate sometimes, set in his ways.

God had a hard time holding Paul to *His*

plans. Paul had some of his own. We can all easily understand that. In the sixteenth chapter of Acts we read, "They were forbidden by the Holy Spirit to preach the word in Asia" (16:6), coupled with sickness being allowed to overtake him in Galatia where the "forbidding" message came. And again this, "They tried to go into Bithynia, but the Spirit did not permit them" (16:7). Tell me, is this the way the Spirit of God leads? That I should go driving ahead until He must pull me up with a sharp turn and twist me around? It is the way He is obliged to do many times, no doubt, with most of us. But His chosen way? Surely not. Rather this, the keeping close and quiet and listening for the next step. The "I am not yet going up to this feast" of Jesus (John 7:8). And then in a few days going up when the clear intimation came. The words "tried to go," "forbidden," "did not permit"—what flashlights they shine into this strong man's character.

But there is much stronger evidence yet. Paul had an ambition to preach to the *Jerusalem Jews*. It burned in his bones from the early hours of his new life. The substratum of Jerusalem seemed ever in his thoughts and dreams. If *he* could just get to those Jerusalem Jews! He knew them. He had trained with them. He was a leader among the younger set. When they burned against these Christians he burned just a bit hotter. They knew him. They trusted him to drive the opposite wedge. If only *he* could have a chance down there he felt that the tide might be turned. But from that critical hour on the Damascene road "Gentiles" had been sounded in his ears. And of course he obeyed, with all his ardent heart. *But—* those Jerusalem Jews! If he might go to Jerusalem! Yet very early the Master had proscribed the Jerusalem service for Paul. He made it a matter of a special vision in the holy temple, kindly explaining why. "They will not receive your testimony concerning Me" (Acts 22:18). Would that not seem quite sufficient? Surely. Yet this astonishing thing occurs: Paul attempts to argue with the Master *why* he should be allowed to go. The Master closes the vision with a peremptory word of command, "*Depart*, for I will send you far from here [from Jerusalem, where you long to be] to the Gentiles" (Acts 22:21, emphasis added). That is a picture of this man. It reveals the weak side in this giant of strength and love. And *this* is the man God has to use in His plan. He is without doubt the best man available, and in his splendor he stands head and shoulders above his generation and many generations. Yet

(I say this with much reverence) God has a hard time getting Paul to work always along the line of *His* plans.

That is the man. Now for the thorn. Something came into Paul's life that was a constant irritation. He calls it a thorn. What a graphic word! Asleep, awake, stitching tent canvas, preaching, writing, that thing ever cutting its point into his sensitive flesh. It did not disturb him so much at first, because there was God to go to. He went to God and said, "*Please* take this away." But it stayed. A second time the prayer; a bit more urgent; the thing sticks. The time test is the hardest test of all. Still no change. Then praying the third time with what earnestness one can well imagine.

Now note three things: First, *there was an answer*. God answered the man. Though He did not grant the petition, He answered the man. He did not ignore him or his request. Then God told Paul frankly that it was not best to take the thorn away. It was in the lonely vigil of a sleepless night, likely as not, that the wondrous Jesus-Spirit drew near to Paul. "Paul," the voice said, "I know about that thorn—and how it hurts. It hurts Me, too. For *your* sake I would quickly remove it. But Paul, it is a bit better for *others'* sake that it remain; the plan in My heart *through you* for thousands can so best be worked out. I will be so close to your side; you will have such revelations of My glory that the pain will be overlapped; the glory will outstrip the thorn point."

I can see old Paul one night in his own hired house in Rome. It is late, after a busy day. He is sitting on an old bench, slowing down before seeking sleep. One arm is around Luke and the other around Timothy. And with eyes that glisten and voice tremulous with emotion he is saying, "Dear old friends, do you know, I would not have missed this thorn for the wondrous *glory-presence of Jesus* that came with it."

And so out of the experience came a double blessing. There was a much fuller working of God's plan for His poor world. And there was an unspeakable nearness of intimacy with his Lord for Paul. *The man was answered and the petition denied that the larger plan of service might be carried out.*

Shaping a Prayer on the Anvil of the Knees

The last of these pictures is in a room by itself. One enters with a holy hush over his spirit and, with awe, looks at Jesus in Gethsemane. There is the Kidron brook, the gentle rise of ground, the grove of gnarled old olive trees. The moon above is full. Here is a group of men lying on the ground apparently asleep. Over yonder deeper among the trees a smaller group reclines motionless. They, too, sleep. And farther in yet is that lone figure, all alone.

This great Jesus! Son of God, God the Son. God—a man! The union of divine and human is itself divine, and therefore beyond human understanding. Here His humanity stands out, pathetically, luminously. This is holiest ground. The battle of the next is being fought out here. Calvary is in Gethsemane. The victory of the hill is won in the grove.

It is impossible for sinful man to understand the horror with which a sinless one thinks of actual contact with sin. As Jesus entered the grove that night it came in upon His spirit with terrific intensity that He was actually coming into contact with sin. In some way all too deep for definition He was to "be sin for us" (2 Corinthians 5:21). An indescribable horror, a chill of terror seizes Him. The poisonous miasma of sin seems to be filling His nostrils and stifling Him. The agony is upon Him. A bit of that prayer comes to us in tones strangely altered by deepest emotion. *"If it be possible—let this cup pass.*" There is still a clinging to some possibility other than that of this nightmare vision. The strain of spirit almost snaps the life-thread, and a parenthetical prayer for strength goes up. And the angels come with sympathetic strengthening. By and by a calmer mood asserts itself, and out of the darkness a second petition comes. It tells of the tide's turning and the victory full and complete. "*Since this cup may not pass*—since only thus *can* Your great plan for a world be worked out—*Your—will—be—done.*"

The changed prayer was worked out on His knees! There alone with the Father came the clearer understanding of the Father's actual will.

True prayer is worked out on the knees alone with God. Shall we not plan to meet God alone, habitually, with the door shut and the Book open, and the will compliant so we may be trained for this holy partnership of prayer? Then will come the clearer vision, the broader purpose, the truer wisdom, the real unselfishness, the simplicity of claiming and expecting, the delights of fellowship in service with Him; then, too, will come great victories for God in His world.

3

❖

THE GREAT
OUTSIDE HINDRANCE

The Traitor Prince

Satan has the power to hold the answer back—for a while. He has not the power to hold it back finally, *if* someone understands and prays with quiet, steady persistence. The real pitch of prayer therefore is toward Satan.

In the Book he is a being of great beauty, endowed with remarkable intellectual powers, a prince at the head of a remarkable organization that he has wielded with phenomenal skill and success in furthering his ambitious purposes.

It is striking that the oldest and latest of the Bible books, Job and Revelation, the first word and the last, give such definite information concerning him. These, coupled with the Gospel records, supply most of the information available, though not all. Those three and a half years of Jesus' public work is the period of greatest satanic and demonic activity of which any record has been made. Jesus' own allusions to him are frequent and in unmistakable language. There are four particular passages to which I want to turn your attention now. Let it not be supposed, however, that this phase of prayer rests upon a few isolated passages. Such a serious truth does not hinge upon selected proof texts. It is woven into the very texture of this Book.

There are two facts that run through the Bible from one end to the other. One is this—there is an enemy. Turn where you will from Genesis to Revelation—always an enemy. He is smart, subtle, malicious, cruel, and obstinate. He is a master. The second fact is this: the leaders for God have always been men of prayer above everything else. They are men of power in other ways, preachers, men of action, with power to sway others but above all else men of prayer. They give prayer first place.

Praying Is Fighting

But let us turn to the Book at once, For we *know* only what it tells. The rest is surmise. The only authoritative statements about Satan seem to be these here.

Turn to Ephesians. Ephesians is a prayer epistle. That is a very significant fact to mark. Of Paul's thirteen letters, Ephesians stands out as the prayer letter. Paul is clearly in a prayer mood. He is on his knees here. He has much to say to these people whom he has won to Christ, but it comes in the parenthesis of his prayer. The connecting phrase running through is "for this cause I pray. . . . I bow my knees." Halfway through, his mind runs out to the condition of these churches, and he puts in the always needed practical injunctions about their daily lives. Then the prayer mood reasserts itself, and the epistle finds its climax in a remarkable paragraph on prayer. From praying the man urges them to pray.

The main drive of all their living and warfare seems very clear to this scarred veteran: "that you may be able to stand against the wiles of the devil" (Ephesians 6:11). This man seems to have had no difficulty in believing in a personal devil. Probably he had had too many close encounters for that. To Paul Satan is a cunning strategist requiring every bit of available resource to combat.

Who is the real foe? Listen: "For we do not wrestle against flesh and blood, but against principalities"—a word for a compact organization of individuals—"against powers, against the rulers of the darkness of this age, against spiritual hosts of wickedness in the heavenly places"—spirit beings, in vast numbers, having their headquarters somewhere above the earth (Ephesians 6:12). *That* is the foe. In chapter 2 of the epistle the head of this organization is referred to as "the prince of the power of the air" (2:2). That is the real foe.

Then in one of his strong climactic sentences Paul tells how the fight is to be won. This sentence runs unbroken through verses 14 to 20. There are six preliminary clauses in it leading up to its main statement. These clauses name the pieces of armor used by a Roman soldier in the action of battle: the loins girded, the breastplate on, the feet shod, the shield, the helmet, the sword, and so on. A Roman soldier reading this or hearing Paul preach it would expect him to finish the sentence by saying "with all your fighting strength fighting."

That would be the proper conclusion of this sentence. But when Paul reaches the climax with his usual intensity he puts in the thing with which the fighting is done—"*praying* always with all prayer" (Ephesians 6:18, emphasis added). Praying is fighting, spirit-fighting. This old evangelist-missionary-bishop says we are in the thick of a fight. There is a war on. How will we best fight? First get into good shape to pray, and then with all your praying strength and skill *pray*. That word *praying* is the climax of this long sentence, and of this whole epistle. This is the sort of action that turns the enemy's flank and reveals his heels. He simply *cannot* stand before persistent knee-work.

Now mark the keenness of Paul's description of the man who does most effective work in praying. There are six qualifications under the figure of the six pieces of armor. A clear understanding of truth, a clean obedient life, earnest service, a simple trust in God, clear assurance of one's own salvation and relation to God, and a good grip of the truth for others—these things prepare a man for the real conflict of prayer. *Such a man—praying—drives back these hosts of the traitor prince*. Such a man praying is invincible in his Chief, Jesus.

Look at how the strong climax of this long sentence runs. "With all prayer and supplication"—there is *intensity*; "praying"—that is *the main drive*; "always"—*ceaselessness*; "in the Spirit"—as *guided by the Chief*;

"being watchful"—*sleepless vigilance*; "with all perseverance"—*persistence*; "and supplication"—*intensity again*; "for all the saints"—*keep in touch with the whole army*; "and for me"—the human leader, rally around *the immediate leader*. This is the foe to be fought. And this the sort of fighting that defeats this foe.

A Double Wrestling Match

Now let us turn to the story of Daniel. In the tenth chapter, Daniel is an old man now. He is an exile. He has not seen the green hills of his fatherland since boyhood. In this level Babylon, he is heartsick over the plight of his people. He has been studying Jeremiah's prophecies and finds there the promise plainly made that after seventy years these exiled Hebrews are to be allowed to return. The thought of it quickens his pulse. He does some quick counting. The time will soon be up. So Daniel plans a bit of time for special prayer, a sort of siege prayer.

Remember who he is. He is the chief executive of the land. He controls, under the king, the affairs of the world empire of his time. He is a giant of strength and ability. But he plans his work so as to go away for a time. Taking a few kindred spirits who understand prayer, he goes off into the woods down by the great Tigris River. They spend a day in fasting and meditation and prayer.

They are expecting an answer. These old-time intercessors were strong in expectancy. But there is no answer. A second day, a third, a fourth, a week, still no answer reaches them. They go on quietly without hesitation. Two weeks. How long it must have seemed! Think of fourteen days spent *waiting* for something, with your heart on pins and needles. There is no answer. God might have been dead, so far as any answer reaching them is concerned. But you cannot fool Daniel in that way. He is an old hand at prayer. Apparently he has no thought of quitting. He goes quietly, steadily on. Twenty days pass, with no change. Still they persist. Then the twenty-first day comes and there is an answer. It comes in a vision whose glory is beyond human strength to bear. By and by when he and his visitor can talk, this is what Daniel hears: "Daniel, the first day you began to pray, your prayer was heard, and I was sent with the answer." And even Daniel's eyes open big— "the *first* day—three weeks ago?" "Yes, three weeks ago I left the presence of God with the answer to your prayer. But"—here is the strange part—"the prince of the kingdom of Persia withstood me twenty-one days; but Michael, one of the chief princes, came to help me, and I was free to come to you with the answer to your prayer."

Please notice four things that I think anyone reading this chapter will readily admit. This being talking with Daniel is plainly a spirit being. He is opposed by someone. This opponent plainly must be a spirit being, too, to be resisting a spirit being. Daniel's messenger is from God: that is clear. Then the opponent must be from the opposite camp. And here comes in the strange, unexpected thing: the evil spirit being *has the power to detain God's messenger* for three full weeks by earth's reckoning of time. Then reinforcements come, as we would say. The evil messenger's purpose is defeated, and God's messenger is free to come as originally planned.

There is a double scene being enacted: a scene you can see and a scene you cannot see. An unseen wrestling match in the upper spirit realm, and two embodied spirit beings down on their faces by the river. And both concerned over the same thing.

That is the Daniel story. It is a picture glowing with the action of real life. It is a double picture. Every prayer action is in doubles: a lower human level and an upper spirit level. Many see only the seen and lose heart. While we look at the things that are seen, let us gaze intently at the things unseen; for the seen things are secondary, but the unseen are chief, and the action of life is being decided there.

Prayer Concerns Three

Jesus lets in a flood of light on Satan's relation to prayer in one of His prayer parables. There are two parables dealing distinctively with prayer: "the friend at midnight" (see Luke 11:5–13) and "the unjust judge" (see Luke 18:1–8). The second of these deals directly with this Satan phase of prayer. It is Luke through whom we learn most of Jesus' own praying.

It comes along toward the end. The swing has been made from plain talking to the less direct, parable form of teaching. The issue with the national leaders has reached its acutest stage. The culmination of their hatred, short of the cross, found vent in charging Him with being inspired by the spirit of Satan. He felt their charge keenly and answered it directly and fully. His parable of the strong man being bound before his house can be rifled comes in here. *They* had no question as to what that meant. That is the setting of this prayer parable. The setting is a partial interpretation. Let us look at this parable rather closely, for it is full of help for those who desire to become skilled in helping God win His world back home again.

Jesus seems so eager that they not miss the meaning here that He departs from His usual habit and says plainly what this parable is meant to teach: "that men always ought to pray and not lose heart." The great essential, He says, is *prayer*. The great essential in prayer is *persistence*. The temptation in prayer is that one may lose heart and give up, or give in.

There are three people in the parable: a judge, a widow, and an adversary. The judge is utterly selfish, unjust, godless, and reckless of anybody's opinion. The widow—well, she is a widow, the picture of friendlessness and helplessness. This woman has lost her nearest, dearest friend, her protector. She is alone. There is an adversary, an opponent at law, who has unrighteously or illegally gotten an advantage over the widow and is ruthlessly pushing her to the wall. She is seeking to get the judge to join with her against her adversary. Her urgent, oft-repeated request is "avenge me of my adversary." That is Jesus' illustration of persistent prayer.

Let us look into it a little further. *Adversary*

is a common word in scripture for Satan. He is the accuser, the hater, the enemy. Its meaning technically is "an opponent in a suit at law." It is the same word as used later by Peter, "Your adversary the devil walks about like a roaring lion, seeking whom he may devour" (1 Peter 5:8). The word *avenge*, used four times, really means "do me justice." It suggests that the widow has the facts on her side to win a clear case, and that the adversary has been pushing his case through by sheer force.

There is a strange feature to this parable, which must have a meaning. *An utterly godless, unscrupulous man is put in to represent God!* This is startling. With any other than Jesus it would seem an overstepping of the bounds. But there is keenness of a rare sort here. Such a man is chosen for judge to bring out most sharply this point: the sort of thing required to win this judge is certainly not required *with God*. The widow must persist and plead because of the sort of man she has to deal with. But God is utterly different in character. Therefore while persistence is urged in prayer, plainly it is not for the reason that required the widow to persist. And if that reason be cut out it leaves only one other, namely, that represented by the adversary.

Having purposely put such a man in the parable for God, Jesus takes pains to speak of the real character of God. "And He is *long-suffering* over them." *That* is God. That word *long-suffering* and its equivalent on Jesus' lips suggests at once the strong side of love, namely, *patience*. It has bothered the scholars in this phrase to know with whom or over what the long-suffering is exercised. "Over them" is the doubtful phrase. Long-suffering over these praying ones? Or long-suffering in dealing righteously with some stubborn adversary—which? The next sentence has a word set in sharpest contrast with this one, namely *speedily*. "Long-suffering" yet "speedily."

Here are gleams of bright light on a dark subject. Jesus always spoke thoughtfully. He chose His words. Remembering the adversary against whom the persistence is directed, the whole story seems to suggest that there is a great conflict going on in the upper spirit world. Concerning it our patient God is long-suffering. He is a just and righteous God. These beings in the conflict are all His creatures. He is just in His dealings with the devil and this splendid host of evil spirits even as with all His creation. He is long-suffering, that no unfairness should be done in His dealings with these creatures of His. Yet at the same time He is doing His best to bring the conflict to a speedy end, for the sake of His loyal loved ones and that right may prevail.

The upshot of the parable is very plain. It contains for us two tremendous truths. First is this: *prayer concerns three*—God to whom we pray, the man on the contested earth who prays, and the evil one against whom we pray. And the purpose of the prayer is not to persuade or influence God but to join forces with Him against the enemy. Not toward God but with God against Satan—that is the main thing to keep in mind in prayer.

The second intense truth is this: the winning quality in prayer is *persistence*. The final test is here. Many who fight well up to this point lose their grip here and lose all. Many who are well equipped for prayer fail here because they have not rightly understood. With clear, ringing tones the Master's voice sounds in our ears again: "to always pray, *and* not lose heart."

A Stubborn Foe Routed

That is the parable teaching. Now a look at a word from the Master's lips. It is in the story of the demon-possessed boy, the distressed father, and the defeated disciples. The demon's treatment of the possessed boy was malicious to an extreme. His purpose was "to destroy" him. Yet there was a limit to his power, for what he wanted to do was something he was not yet able to do. He showed extreme tenacity. He fought bitterly against being disembodied again. The disciples had tried to cast him out. They were expected to. They expected to. They had before. They failed!—dismally.

Then Jesus came. His presence changed all. The demon angrily left, doing his worst to wreck the house he had to vacate. The boy was restored and the crowd astonished at the power of God.

Then the disciples did an important thing. They sought a private talk with Jesus. No shrewder thing was ever done. When you fail, quit your service and get away for a private interview with Jesus. With eyes big and voices dejected, the question wrung itself out of their sinking hearts: "Why could *we* not cast it out?" Matthew and Mark together supply the full answer. Probably first came this: "because of your unbelief" (Matthew 17:20). They had quaked in their hearts before the power of the malicious demon, and the demon knew it. They were more impressed with the power of the demon than with the power of God. They had not prayed victoriously against the demon. The Master says,

"If you have faith as a mustard seed, you will say to this mountain, 'Move from here to there'" (Matthew 17:20). Note that the direction of the faith is toward the obstacle. Its force is against the enemy. It was the demon who was most directly influenced by Jesus' faith.

Then comes the second part of the reply: "This kind can come out by nothing but prayer and fasting" (Mark 9:29). Some less stubborn demons may be cast out by the faith that comes of our regular prayer-touch with God, but this extreme sort takes special prayer. It can be put out by nothing less. The real victory must be in the secret place. The exercise of faith in the open battle is then a mere pressing of the victory already won. These men had the language of Jesus on their lips, but they had not first gotten the victory somewhere alone. This demon was determined not to go. He fought stubbornly and strongly and succeeded. Then this *Man of prayer* came. The quiet word of command was spoken. The demon had to go. These disciples were strikingly like some of us. They had not realized where the real victory is won. They had used the word of command to the demon, doubtless coupling Jesus' name with it. But there was not the secret touch with God that gives victory.

Their eyes showed their fear of the demon.

Real, intelligent prayer is what routs Satan's demons, for it routs their chief. David killed the lion and bear in the secret forests before he faced the giant in the open. These disciples were facing the giant in the open without the discipline in secret. "This kind can come out by nothing but prayer" means this: "This kind comes out, and must come out, before the man who prays." This thing that Jesus calls prayer casts out demons. It exerts a positive influence on the hosts of evil spirits. They fear it. They fear the man who becomes skilled in its use.

There are many other passages in the Bible fully as explicit as these. The very language of scripture is full of this truth. But these four great instances are quite sufficient to make the present point clear and plain. This great renegade prince is an actual active factor in the lives of men. He believes in the potency of prayer. He fears it. He can hinder its results for a while. He does his best to hinder it, and to hinder as long as possible.

Prayer overcomes him. It defeats his plans and himself. He cannot successfully stand before it. He trembles when some man of simple faith in God prays. Prayer is insistence upon God's will being done. It needs for its practice a man in sympathetic touch with God. Its basis is Jesus' victory. It overcomes the opposing will of the great traitor-leader.

III.

How to Pray

1

The "How" of Relationship

God's Ambassadors

If I had an ambition to be an ambassador to England, there would be two essential things involved. The first essential would be to receive the appointment. I would need to have a relationship with our president, possess certain qualifications considered essential by him, and secure from his hand the appointment and the official credentials of my appointment. That would establish my relationship to the foreign court as the representative of my own country, and my right to transact business in her name.

But having gotten that far I might go over there and make bad mistakes. I might get our diplomatic relations tangled up, requiring many explanations and maybe apologies, and leaving unpleasant memories for a long time to come.

Such incidents have not been infrequent. Nations are very sensitive. Governmental affairs must be handled with great diplomacy. There would be a second thing that, if I were a wise enough man to be an ambassador, I would likely do. I would go to see several experienced ambassadors and have as many interviews with them as possible, learning all I possibly could from them of London official life, court etiquette, personages to be dealt with, things to do, and things to avoid. How to be a successful diplomat and further the good feeling between the two governments and win friends for our country among the sturdy Britons would be my one absorbing thought. And having gotten all I could in that way I would be constantly on the alert with all the mental keenness I could command to practice being a successful ambassador.

The first of these would make me technically an ambassador. The second would tend toward giving me some skill as an ambassador. Now there are the same two hows in praying. First the relationship must be established before any business can be transacted. Then skill must be acquired in the transacting of the business at hand.

Right now let's talk about the first of these,

the how of relationship in prayer. The basis of prayer is right relationship with God. Prayer is representing God in the spirit realm of this world. It is insisting upon His rights down in this sphere of action. It is standing for Him with full powers from Him. Clearly the only basis of such relationship to God is *Jesus*. We have been outlawed by sin. We were in touch with God. We broke with Him. The break could not be repaired by us. Jesus came. He was God *and* Man. He touches both. We get back only through Him. The blood of the cross is the basis of all prayer. Through it the relationship is established that underlies all prayer. Only as I come to God through Jesus to get the sin score straightened, and only as I keep in sympathy with Jesus in the purpose of my life, can I practice prayer.

Six Sweeping Statements

Jesus' own words make this very clear. There are two groups of teachings on prayer in those three and a half years as given by the Gospel records. The first of these groups is in the Sermon on the Mount, and the second group comes at the end of His life.

It is after the sharp rupture with the leaders that this second series of statements is made. The most positive and most sweeping utterances on prayer are here. Of Jesus' eight promises regarding prayer, six are here. Let's take a look at these six promises and then notice their relationship to our topic of today.

The first of these is in Matthew 18:19–20: "Again I say to you that if two of you agree on earth concerning anything that they ask, it will be done for them by My Father in heaven." Notice the place of prayer—"on earth"; and the sweep—"anything"; and the certainty—"it will be done." Then the reason is given. "For where two or three are gathered together in My name, I am there in the midst of them." That is to say, if there are two persons praying, there are three. There is always one more than you can see. And if you might perhaps be saying to yourself in a bit of dejection, "He won't hear me; I'm so sinful, so weak," you would be wrong in thinking and saying so. *If* you might be thinking that, you could at once fall back upon this: the Father always hears Jesus. And wherever earnest hearts pray, Jesus is there taking their prayer and making it His prayer.

The second of these is Mark 11:22–24: "Jesus answered and said to them, 'Have faith in God.'" The chief factor in prayer is God. "'For assuredly, I say to you, whoever says to this mountain, "Be removed and cast into the sea. . ."'" He chose the most unlikely thing that could occur. Such a thing did not take place. We never hear of Jesus moving an actual mountain. The need for such action does not seem to have arisen. But He chooses the thing most difficult for His illustration. "'. . .and does not doubt in his heart'"—that is Jesus' definition of faith— "'but believes that those things he says will be done, he will have whatever he says. Therefore I say to you, whatever things you ask when you pray, believe that you receive them, and you will have them.'" How utterly sweeping this last statement! Both whatever and whoever are here. Anything and anybody.

The last four of the six are in John's Gospel. In John 14:13–14 we read, "And whatever you ask in My name, that I will do, that the Father may be glorified in the Son. If you ask anything in My name, I will do it." The repetition is to emphasize the unlimited sweep of what may be asked.

John 15:7 says: "If you abide in Me, and My words abide in you, you will ask what you desire" —there is nothing said directly about God's will; there is something said about our wills— "and it shall be done for you." Or, a little more literally, "I will bring it to pass for you."

This same chapter, verse 16, says: "You did not choose Me, but I chose you and appointed you that you should go and bear fruit, and that your fruit should remain, that whatever you ask the Father in My name He may give you." God had our prayer partnership with Himself in His mind in choosing us. And the last of these, John 16:23–24, says, "Most assuredly, I say to you, whatever you ask the Father in My name He will give you. Until now you have asked nothing in My name. Ask, and you will receive, that your joy may be full."

These statements are the most sweeping to be found anywhere in the scriptures regarding prayer. There is no limitation as to who shall ask, nor about the kind of thing to be asked for. There are three limitations imposed: the prayer is to be *through Jesus*; the person praying is to be in fullest sympathy with Him; and this person is to have faith.

Words with a Freshly Honed Razor Edge

Now please group these six sweeping statements in your mind and hold them together there. Then notice carefully this fact. These words are not spoken to the crowds. They are spoken to the small inner group of twelve disciples. Jesus talks one way to the multitude. He oftentimes talks differently to these men who have separated themselves from the crowd and come into the inner circle.

And notice further that before Jesus spoke these words to this group of men He had said something else first, something so radical that it led to a sharp passage between Himself and Peter, to whom He spoke very sternly. This something else fixes unmistakably their relationship to Himself. Remember that the sharp break with the national leaders had come. Jesus was charged with satanic collusion. The death plot was determined upon. And now the Master was frequently slipping away from the crowd with these twelve men and seeking to teach and train them. That is the setting of these great promises. It must be kept continually in mind.

Before the Master gave Himself away to these men in these promises He said something else. It is this: "If anyone desires to come after Me, let him deny himself, and take up his cross, and follow Me" (Matthew 16:24). *These words should be written crosswise over those six prayer statements.* Those six promises are not meant for all. They are meant only for those who will square their lives by these razor-edged words.

"If anyone desires to come after Me" means a rock-rooted purpose; the jaw locked; the tendrils of the purpose going down under the gray granite of a person's will and tying themselves there, and knotting the ties.

"Come after Me" means all the power of Jesus' life, as well as the wilderness, the intense temptation. It may mean the obscure village of Nazareth for you. It may mean that first Judean year for you—lack of appreciation. It may mean for you that last six months—the desertion of those hitherto friendly. It will mean without doubt a Gethsemane. Everybody who comes along after Jesus has a Gethsemane in his life. It will never mean as much to you as it meant to Him. That is true. But, then, it will mean everything to you. And it will also mean having a Calvary in your life in a very real sense, though different from what that meant to Him. This sentence gives the process whereby man may come into such relationship with God as to claim without any reservation these great prayer promises. And if that sounds hard and severe to you, let me quickly say that it is an easy way for the man who is *willing*. The presence of Jesus in the life overlaps every cutting thing.

If a man will go through Matthew 16:24 and

habitually live there, he may ask what he wills to ask, and that thing will come to pass. The reason, without question, why many people do not have power in prayer is simply because they are unwilling to bare their hearts to the keen-edged knife in these words of Jesus. And on the other side, if a man will quietly, resolutely follow the Master's leading day by day, he will be startled to find what an utterly new meaning prayer will come to have for him.

The Controlling Purpose

Vital relationship is always expressed by purpose. The wise ambassador has an absorbing purpose to further the interests of his government. Jesus said, "I always do those things that please Him."

The relationship that underlies prayer has an absorbing, controlling purpose: to please Jesus. That sentence may sound simple enough, but there is no sentence I might utter that has a more freshly honed razor edge to it than that. The purpose that *controls* my action in every matter is this: to please Him. If you have not done so, take it for a day, a week, and use it as a touchstone regarding thought, word, and action. Take it into matters personal, home, business, social, fraternal. It does not mean to ask, "Is this right? Is this wrong?" Not that. There are a great many things that can be proven to not be wrong but that are not best, that are not His preference.

It will make one think of his personal habits, his business methods and social interactions, the organizations he belongs to, with the quiet question cutting its razor way into each.

If someone asks, "Why put the condition of prayer so strongly as that?" I will remind you of this. The true basis of prayer is sympathy, oneness of purpose. Prayer is not extracting favors from a reluctant God. It is not passing a check in a bank window for money. That is mandatory. The roots of prayer lie in oneness of purpose. God up yonder, His Victor-Son by His side, and a man down here, in *such sympathetic touch* that God can think His thoughts in this man's mind and have His desires repeated upon the earth as this man's prayer.

The Threefold Cord of Jesus' Life
Think for a moment about Jesus' human life down here: His marvelous activities over which the world has never ceased to wonder, then His hidden-away prayer life of which only occasional glimpses are gotten. Then grouping around that sentence of His in John's Gospel—"I do always

the things that are pleasing to Him"—notice the "nots" on Jesus' lips: not My will, not My works, not My words. Jesus came to do somebody's else will. The controlling purpose of His life was to please His Father. That was the secret of the power of His earthly career. Right relationship to God, an intimate prayer-life, marvelous power over men and with men—those are the strands in the threefold cord of His life.

There is a striking turn of a word in the second chapter of John's Gospel. "Many believed in His name when they saw the signs which He did. But Jesus did not commit Himself to them" (John 2:23–24) because He knew them so well. The words *believed* and *commit* are the same word underneath our English. The sentence might better run, "Many *trusted* Him when they saw the miracles that He did; but He did not *trust* them for He knew them." I have no doubt most of us trust Him. But can He trust you? While we might all shrink from saying yes to that, there is a very real sense in which we may say yes, namely, in the purpose of the life. Every life is controlled by some purpose. What is yours? To please Him? If so, He knows it. It is a great comfort to remember that God judges a man not by his achievements but by his purposes: not by what

I am in actuality but by what I desire to be, in the yearning of my inmost heart, the dominant purpose of my life. God will fairly flood your life with all the power He can trust you to use wholly for Him.

The person who will live in Matthew 16:24 and follow Jesus as He leads day by day—simply that, no fanaticism, no extremism—then those six promises of Jesus with their limitless sweep are his to use as he will.

2

❖

The "How" of Method

Touching the Hidden Keys

One of the most remarkable illustrations of the power of prayer may be found in an experience of D. L. Moody. It explains his unparalleled career of worldwide soul winning. One marvels that more has not been said of it. Its stimulus to faith is great. I suppose the man most concerned did not speak of it much because of his humility. The last year of his life he referred to it more frequently as though impelled to.

The last time I heard Mr. Moody was in his own church in Chicago. It was, I think, in the fall of the last year of his life. In a quiet conversational way he told the story.

Back in the early 1870s he went to London to learn what he could from preachers there, so as to do better work here. He had not been speaking anywhere but listening to others. One Saturday at noon he had gone into a meeting in Exeter Hall on the Strand. He felt compelled to speak a little when the meeting was thrown open, and did so. At the close, a minister asked him to come and preach for him the next day, and he said he would. Mr. Moody said, "I went to the morning service and found a large church full of people. And when the time came I began to speak to them. But it seemed the hardest talking I ever did. There was no response in their faces. They seemed as though carved out of stone or ice. I was having a hard time and wished I wasn't there and wished I hadn't promised to speak again at night. But I had promised, and so I went.

"At night it was the same thing: house full, people outwardly respectful, but no interest, no response. And I was having a hard time again. About halfway through my talk there came a change. It seemed as though the windows of heaven had opened and a bit of breath blew down. The atmosphere of the building seemed to change. The people's faces changed. It impressed me so that when I finished speaking I gave the invitation for those who wanted to be Christians to rise. I thought there might be a few. And to my immense surprise the people got up in groups, pew-fulls. I turned to the minister and said,

'What does this mean?' He said, 'I don't know.'

"Well," Mr. Moody said, "they misunderstood me. I'll explain what I meant." So he announced an after-meeting in the room below, explaining who were invited—only those who wanted to be Christians—and dismissed the service.

They went to the lower room. And the people came crowding in, filling every available space. Mr. Moody talked a few minutes and then asked those who wanted to be Christians to rise. This time he knew he had made his meaning clear. They got up in groups, by fifties! Mr. Moody said, "I turned and said to the minister, 'What *does* this mean?' He said, 'I'm sure I don't know.'" Then the minister said to Mr. Moody, "What'll I do with these people? I don't know what to do with them; this is something new." And he said, "Well, I'd announce a meeting for tomorrow night and Tuesday night, and see what comes of it; I'm going across the channel to Dublin." And he went, but he had barely stepped off the boat when a cablegram was handed him from the minister saying, "Come back at once. Church packed." So he went back and stayed ten days. And the result of that ten days was that four hundred were added to that church, and that every church nearby felt the impulse of those ten days. Then Mr. Moody dropped his head, as though thinking back, and said: "I had no plans beyond this church. I supposed my life work was here. But the result with me was that I was given a roving commission and have been working under it ever since."

Now what was the explanation for that marvelous Sunday and days following? It was not Mr. Moody's doing, though he was a leader whom God could and did mightily use. It was not the minister's doing, for he was as greatly surprised as the leader. There was some secret hidden beneath the surface of those ten days. With his usual keenness Mr. Moody set himself to ferret it out.

By and by this incident came to him. A woman in the church had gotten sick some time before. Gradually she grew worse, until the physician told her that she would not recover. She would not die at once, but she would be a shut-in for years. She lay there trying to think what that meant: to be shut in for years. And she thought of her life and said, "How little I've done for God, practically nothing; and now what can I do shut in here on my back?" And she said, "I can pray. I *will* pray." And she was led to pray for her church. Her sister, also a member of the church, lived with her and was her link with the outer world. Sundays, after church service, the sick woman would ask, "Any special interest in church today?" "No," was the constant reply. Wednesday nights, after prayer meetings, "Any special interest in the service tonight? There must have been." "No; nothing new; same old deacons made the same old prayers."

But one Sunday noon the sister came in from service and asked, "Who do you think preached today?" "I don't know, who?" "Why, a stranger from America, a man called Moody, I think was the name." And the sick woman's face turned a bit whiter and her lip trembled a bit, and she quietly said: "I know what that means. There's something coming to the old church. Don't bring me any dinner. I must spend this afternoon in prayer." And so she did. And that night in the service that startling change came.

Then to Mr. Moody himself, as he sought her out in her sickroom, she told how nearly two years before there came into her hands a copy of a paper published in Chicago called the *Watchman* that contained a talk by Mr. Moody in one of the Chicago meetings. All she knew was that talk made her heart burn, and there was the name Moody. And she was led to pray that God would send that man into their church in London. As simple a prayer as that.

The months went by, and a year, and more; still she prayed. Nobody knew of it but herself and God. No change seemed to come. Still she prayed. And of course her prayer wrought its purpose. Every Spirit-suggested prayer does. The Spirit of God moved that man of God across the water to London and into their church. Then a bit of special siege-prayer, and that night the victory came.

I believe without a doubt that someday when the night is gone and the morning light comes up, we shall find that the largest single factor in that ten days' work and in the changing of tens of thousands of lives under Moody's leadership is that woman in her praying. Not the only factor, mind you. Moody was a man of rare leadership and consecration, and hundreds of faithful ministers and others rallied to his support. But behind and beneath Moody and the others, and to be reckoned with as first, was this woman's praying.

Making God's Purpose Our Prayer

Let me suggest a bit of how to pray.

The first thing in prayer is to find God's

purpose; the second thing is to make that purpose our prayer. We want to find out what God is thinking and then claim that which will be done. God is seated on the throne. Jesus Christ is sitting by His side glorified. Everywhere in the universe God's will is being done except in the earth and its atmosphere and that bit of the heavens above it where Satan's headquarters are.

It has been done down here by one person— Jesus. He came here to this prodigal planet and did God's will perfectly. He went away and has sought and seeks to have people on the earth so fully in touch with Himself that He may do in them and through them just what He will, that He may reproduce Himself in these men and have God's will done again down on the earth. Now prayer is this: finding out God's purpose for our lives and for the earth and insisting that that will be done here. The great thing then is to find out and insist on God's will. And the "how" of method in prayer is concerned with that.

Many times I have met with a group of people for prayer. Various special matters for prayer are brought up. Here is this man, needing prayer, and this particular matter, and this one, and this. Then we kneel and pray. And I have many a time thought as I have listened to their prayers as though this is the prayer I must offer: "Blessed Holy Spirit, You know this man and what is lacking in him. There is trouble there. Pray in me the prayer You are praying for this man. The prayer You are praying, I pray that, in Jesus' name. Your will be done here under these circumstances."

Sometimes I feel clear about the particular prayer to offer, but many times I am puzzled to know. I may not know *all* the facts. I know this man who evidently needs prayer, a Christian man perhaps, but there may be some fact in there I do not know that seriously affects the whole difficulty. And I am compelled to fall back on this: I don't know how to pray as I ought, but the Spirit within me will make intercession for this man as I allow Him to have full sway in me as the conduit of His prayer. And He who is listening above as He hears His will for this man being repeated down on the battlefield will recognize His own purpose, and so that thing will be working out because of Jesus' victory over the evil one.

But I may become so sensitive to the Spirit's thoughts and presence that I will know more keenly and quickly what to pray for. Insofar as I do I become a more skillful partner of His on the earth in getting God's will done.

The Rendezvous

There are six suggestions here on how to pray. First, we need *time* for prayer, unhurried, daily time. I do not mean rising in the morning at the very last moment and dressing hurriedly, and then kneeling a few moments so as to feel easier in mind. I do not mean the last thing at night when you are exhausted and almost between the sheets, and then remember and look up a verse and kneel a few moments. That is good so far as it goes. I am not criticizing that. Better sweeten and sandwich the day with all of that sort you can get in. But right now I mean this: *taking time* to thoughtfully pray when the mind is fresh and alert and the spirit sensitive. We haven't time. Life is so crowded. It must be taken from something else, something important, but still less important than this.

Sacrifice is the continual law of life. The important thing must be sacrificed to the more important. One needs to cultivate a mature judgment or his strength will fizzle out in the less important details and the greater thing go undone, or be done poorly. If we would become skilled intercessors and know how to pray simply enough, we must take quiet time daily to get off alone.

The second suggestion: We need a *place* for prayer. Oh, you can pray anywhere, but you are not likely to unless you have been off in some quiet place shut in alone with God. The Master said, "Go into your room, and when you have shut your door"—that door is important; it shuts out and it shuts in—"pray to your Father who is in the secret place" (Matthew 6:6). God is here in this shut-in spot. One must get alone to find out that he is never alone. The more alone we are as far as people are concerned, the least alone we are so far as God is concerned.

The quiet place and time are needful to train the ears for keen hearing. A quiet place shuts out the outer sounds and gives the inner ear a chance to learn other sounds.

A man was standing in a telephone booth trying to talk but could not make out the message. He kept saying, "I can't hear!" The other man finally said sharply, "If you'll shut that door you can hear." *His* door was shut and he could hear not only the man's voice but the street and store noises, too. Some folks have gotten their hearing badly confused because their doors have not been shut enough. Man's voice and God's voice get mixed in their ears. They cannot distinguish between them. The problem is partly with the door. If you'll shut that door you can hear.

The third suggestion needs much emphasis today: *Give the Book of God its place in prayer*. Prayer is not talking to God—simply. It is listening first, then talking. Prayer needs three organs of the head: an ear, a tongue, and an eye. First an ear to hear what God says, then a tongue to speak, then an eye to watch for the result. Bible study is the listening side of prayer. The purpose of God comes in through the ear, passes through the heart, taking on the tinge of your personality, and goes out at the tongue as prayer. It is pathetic what a time God has getting a hearing down here. He is ever speaking, but even where there may be some inclination to hear, the sounds of earth are choking out the sound of His voice. God speaks in His Word. The most we know of God comes to us here. This Book is God in print. God Himself speaks in this Book. Studying it keenly, intelligently, reverently will reveal God's great will. What He says will utterly change what you say.

Our Prayer Teacher

The fourth suggestion is this: *Let the Spirit teach you how to pray*. The more you pray, the more you will find yourself saying to yourself, "I don't know how to pray." God understands that and has a plan to cover our need there. There is One who is a master intercessor. He understands praying perfectly. He is the Spirit of prayer. God has sent Him down to live inside you and me, partly to teach us the fine art of prayer. Let Him teach you.

When you go alone in the quiet time and place with the Book, quietly pray: "Blessed Prayer Spirit, teach me how to pray," and He will. Do not be nervous, wondering if you will understand. Study to be quiet. Be still and listen.

You will find your praying changing. You will talk more simply. You will quit asking for some things. Some of the old forms of prayer will likely drop from your lips. You will use fewer words maybe, but they will be spoken with a quiet, absolute faith that this thing you are asking is being worked out.

This thing of *letting the Spirit teach* must come first in one's praying, remain to the last, and continue all along as the leading dominant factor. The highest law of the Christian life is obedience to the leading of the Holy Spirit. There needs to be a cultivated judgment in reading His leading and not mistaking our haphazard thoughts as His voice. He should be allowed to teach us how to pray, and more—to dominate our praying. The whole range and intensity of the spirit conflict is under His eye. He is God's general on the field of action. There come crises in the battle when the turn of the tide wavers. He knows when a bit of special praying is needed to turn the tide and bring victory. So there needs to be special seasons of persistent prayer, a continuing until victory is assured. Obey His promptings. Sometimes there comes an impulse to pray or to ask another to pray. And we think, *I have just been praying*, or *He prays about this anyway. It is not necessary to pray again. I do not want to suggest it.* Better obey the impulse quietly, with few words of explanation to the other one concerned, or no words beyond simply the request.

Let this wondrous Holy Spirit teach you how to pray. It will take time. You may be a bit set in your way, but if you will just yield and patiently wait, He will teach you what to pray, suggest definite things, and often give you the very language of prayer.

You will notice that the chief purpose of these four suggestions is to learn God's will. The quiet place, the quiet time, the Book, the Spirit—this is the schoolroom. Here we learn His will. Learning that makes one eager to have it done and breathes new life into the longing prayer that it may be done.

There is a fine word much used in the Psalms and in Isaiah for this sort of thing—*waiting*. Over and over again that is the word used for the contact with God that reveals to us His will and imparts to us anew His desires. It is a word full of richest and deepest meaning. Waiting is not an occasional or hurried thing. It means *steadfastness*, that is holding on; *patience*, that is holding back; *expectancy*, that is holding the face up to see; *obedience*, that is holding one's self in readiness to go or do; *listening*, that is holding quiet and still so as to hear.

The Power of a Name

The fifth suggestion has already been referred to but should be repeated here. Prayer must be *in Jesus' name*. The relationship of prayer is through Jesus. And the prayer itself must be offered in His name, because the whole strength of the case lies in Jesus. Let us distinctly bear in mind that we have no standing with God except through Jesus.

As we come in Jesus' name, it is the same as though Jesus prayed. It is the same as though Jesus put His arm in yours and took you up to the Father and said, "Father, here is a friend of Mine; we're on good terms. Please give him anything he asks, for My sake." And the Father would quickly bend over and graciously say, "What'll you have? You may have anything you ask when My Son asks for it." That is the practical effect of asking in Jesus' name.

In the ultimate analysis the force of using Jesus' name is that He is the victor over the traitor prince. Prayer is repeating the Victor's name in the ears of Satan and insisting upon his retreat. As one prays persistently in Jesus' name, the evil one must go.

The Birthplace of Faith

The sixth suggestion is a familiar one, and yet one much misunderstood. Prayer must be *in faith*. But please note that faith here is not believing that God *can* but that He *will*. It is kneeling and making the prayer and then saying, "Father, I thank You for this; that it will be so, I thank You." Then rising and going about your duties, saying, "That thing is settled." Repeating the prayer with the thanks, and then saying as you go off, "That matter is assured." Not going repeatedly to persuade God but understanding that prayer is the deciding factor in a spirit conflict and each prayer is like a fresh blow between the eyes of the enemy.

"Well," someone will say, "can we all have faith like that? Can a man *make* himself believe?" There should be no unnatural mechanical insisting that you do believe. Some earnest people make a mistake there. We will not all have faith like that. I can easily tell you why. The faith that believes that God *will* do what you ask is not born in a hurry; it is not born in the dust of the street and the noise of the crowd. But I can tell where that faith will have a birthplace and keep growing stronger: in every heart that habitually takes quiet time with God and listens to His voice in His Word. Into that heart will come a simple strong faith that the thing it is led to ask will be accomplished.

That faith has four simple characteristics. It is *intelligent*. It finds out what God's will is. Faith is never contrary to reason. Sometimes it is a bit higher up; the reasoning process has not yet reached it. Second, it is *obedient*. It fits its life into God's will. There is apt to be a stiff rub here all the time. Then it is *expectant*. It looks out for the result. It bows down upon the earth but sends a man to keep an eye on the sea. And then it is *persistent*. It hangs on. It says, "Go again seven times, seventy times seven." It reasons that having learned God's will and knowing that He does not change, the delay must be caused by the third person, the enemy, and that stubborn persistence in the Victor's name routs him and leaves a clear field.

3

❖

THE LISTENING
SIDE OF PRAYER

A Trained Ear

In prayer the ear is an organ of first importance.
It is of equal importance with the tongue but
must be named first. Through the ear comes the
use of the tongue. Where the faculties are normal
the tongue is trained only through the ear. This
is nature's method. The mind is molded largely
through the ear and eye. It reveals itself and
asserts itself largely through the tongue. What the
ear lets in, the mind works over and the tongue
gives out.

This is the order in Isaiah's fiftieth chapter in
those words prophetic of Jesus. "The Lord GOD
has given Me the tongue of the learned. . . . He
awakens My ear to hear as the learned" (Isaiah
50:4). Here the taught tongue came through the
awakened ear. One reason so many of us do not

understand tongues is because we give God so little chance to get at our ears.

It is a striking fact that the men who have been mightiest in prayer have known God well. They have seemed uniquely sensitive to Him and overawed with the sense of His love and greatness. There are three Old Testament characters who are particularly mentioned as being mighty in prayer. Jeremiah said that when God spoke to him about the deep perversity of that nation He exclaimed, "Even if Moses and Samuel stood before Me, My mind would not be favorable toward this people" (Jeremiah 15:1). When James wanted an illustration of a man of prayer for the scattered Jews, he spoke of Elijah and one particular crisis in his life, the praying on Carmel's tip-top. These three men are Israel's great men in the great crises of its history. Moses was the maker and molder of the nation. Samuel was the patient teacher who introduced a new order of things in the national life. Elijah was the rugged leader when the national worship of Jehovah was about to be officially overthrown. These three men—the maker, the teacher, the emergency leader—are singled out in the record as men of prayer.

Now regarding these men it is interesting to observe what *listeners* they were to God's voice.

Their ears were trained early and trained long, until great acuteness and sensitivity to God's voice was the result. Special pains seem to have been taken with the first man, the nation's greatest giant and history's greatest jurist. There were two distinct stages in the training of Moses' ears. The first stage of his prayer training was wearing the noise of Egypt out of his ears so he could hear the fine tones of God's voice. He who would become skilled in prayer must take a silence course in the University of Arabia. Then came the second stage. Forty years were followed by forty days, twice over, of listening to God's speaking voice up in the mount. Such an ear-course as that made a skilled famous intercessor.

Samuel had an earlier course than Moses. While yet a child, before his ears had been dulled by earth sounds, they were tuned to the hearing of God's voice. The child heart and ear naturally open upward. They hear easily and believe readily. This child's ear was quickly trained to recognize God's voice. And the tented Hebrew nation soon came to know that there was a man in their midst to whom God was talking.

Of the third of these famous intercessors little is known except of the few striking events in which he figured. Of these, the scene that finds its climax in the opening on Carmel's top of the rain windows occupies by far the greater space. And it is notable that the beginning of that long eighteenth chapter of 1 Kings that tells of the Carmel conflict begins with a message to Elijah from God: "'The word of the Lord came to Elijah. . .I will send rain on the earth.'" That was the foundation of that persistent praying and sevenfold watching on the mountaintop. First the ear heard, then the voice persistently claimed, then the eye expectantly looked. First the voice of God, then the voice of man. That is the true order. Tremendous results always follow that combination.

Through the Book to God
With us the training is of the *inner* ear. And its first training, after the early childhood stage is passed, must usually be through the eye. What God has spoken to others has been written down for us. We hear through our eyes. The eye opens the way to the inner ear. God spoke in His Word. He is still speaking in it and through it. The whole thought here is to get *to know God*. He reveals Himself in the word that comes from His own lips and through His messengers' lips. He reveals Himself in His dealings with men. Every

incident and experience of these pages is a mirror held up to God's face. In them we may come to see Him.

This is studying the Bible not for the Bible's sake but for the purpose of knowing God. The object aimed at is not the Book but the God revealed in the Book.

There is a fascinating story told of one of David's mighty men. One day there was a sudden attack on the camp by the Philistines when the fighting men were all away. This man was there alone. The Philistines were the traditional enemy. The very word *Philistines* struck terror to the Hebrew heart. But this man was reckoned one of the first three of David's mighty men because of his conduct that day. He quietly, quickly gripped his sword and fought the enemy single-handed. Up and down, left and right, hip and thigh he smote with such terrific drive that the enemy turned and fled. And we are told that the muscles of his hand became so rigid around the handle of his sword that he could not tell by the feeling where his hand stopped and the sword began. Man and sword were one that day in the action of service against the nation's enemy. When we so absorb this Book and the Spirit of Him who is its life that people cannot tell the line of division between the man and the God within the man, then will we have mightiest power as God's intercessors in defeating the foe. God and man will be as one in the action of service against the enemy.

A Spirit-Illumined Mind

I want to make some simple suggestions for studying this Book so as to get to God through it. First there must be the *time* element. One must get at least a half hour daily when the mind is fresh. A tired mind does not readily *absorb*. This should be persisted in until there is a habitual spending of at least that much time daily over the Book, with a spirit at leisure from all else so it can take in. Then the time should be given to *the Book itself*. If other books are consulted and read, let that be *after* the reading of this Book. Let God talk to you directly, rather than through somebody else. Give Him first chance at your ears. This Book in the central place of your table, the others grouped about it.

A third suggestion brings out the circle of this work. *Read prayerfully*. We learn how to pray by reading prayerfully. This Book does not reveal its sweetness and strength to the sharp mind merely but to the Spirit-enlightened mind.

There is a fourth word to put in here. We must read *thoughtfully*. Fight shallowness. Insist on reading thoughtfully. A word in the Bible for this is *meditate*. Run through and pick out this word with its variations. The word underneath that English word means "to mutter," as though a man were repeating something over and over again as he turned it over in his mind. We have another word with the same meaning that is not used much now—*ruminate*. We call the cow a ruminant because she chews the cud. She will spend hours chewing the cud and then give us the rich milk that she has extracted from her food. That is the word here—*ruminate*. Chew the cud if you want to get the richest cream and butter.

There is a fifth suggestion that is easier to make than to follow. *Read obediently*. As the truth appeals to your conscience, *let it change your habit and life*.

Jesus gives the law of knowledge in His famous words: "If anyone wills to do His will, he shall know concerning the doctrine" (John 7:17). If we do what we know to do, we will know more. If we know to do and hesitate and do not obey, the inner eye will surely go blind and the sense of right be dulled and lost. Obedience to truth is the eye of the mind.

Wide Reading

Then one needs to have a *plan* of reading. A consecutive plan gathers up the fragments of time into a strong whole. Get a good plan and stick to it. Better a fairly good plan faithfully followed than the best plan if used only occasionally. All the numerous methods of study can probably be grouped under three general heads: wide reading, topical study, and textual. We all do some textual study in a more or less small way: digging into a sentence or verse to get at its true and deep meaning. We probably all do some topical study: gathering up statements on some one subject, studying a character. The more pretentious name is biblical theology, finding and arranging all that is taught in the whole range of the Bible on any one theme.

But I want to especially urge *wide reading* as being the basis of all study. It is the simple, the natural, the scientific method. It is adapted to all classes of persons. It is *the* method of all for all. It underlies all methods of getting a grasp of this wonderful Book and so coming to as full an understanding of God as is possible.

By wide reading is meant a *rapid reading through* regardless of verse, chapter, or book divisions. Reading it as *a narrative*, a story, as you would read any book. There will be a reverence of spirit with this book that no other inspires, but with the same intellectual method of running through to see what is here. No book is so fascinating as the Bible when read this way.

To illustrate, begin at Genesis and read rapidly through *by the page*. Do not try to understand all. You won't. Just push on. Do not try to remember everything. Do not think about that. Let stick to you what will. You will be surprised to find how much will. You may read ten or twelve pages in your first half hour. Next time start in where you left off. You may get through Genesis in three or four sessions, more or less, depending on your mood and how fast your habit of reading may be.

But do not stop at the close of Genesis. Push on into Exodus. The connection is immediate. It is the same book. And so on into Leviticus. Now do not try to understand Leviticus the first time, but you can easily group its contents into the offerings, the law of offerings, incidents, and sanitary regulations. And in it all you will be getting the picture of God—*that is the point*. And so on through the Bible.

A second stage of this wide reading is fitting together the parts. The arrangement of our Bible is not chronological but topical. For example, open your Bible to the close of Esther and again at the close of Malachi. The books from Genesis to Esther we know as the historical section, and this second section the poetical and prophetical section. There is some history in the prophecy, and some prophecy and poetry in the historical part, but in the main the first part is historical and the second poetry and prophecy. These two parts belong together. Fit the poetry and the prophecy into the history. Do it on your own, as though it had never been done. It has been done much better than you will do it, and you will make some mistakes. You can check them afterward in some scholarly books. You cannot tell where some parts belong, but meanwhile the thing to note is this: You are absorbing the Book. It is becoming a part of you. There is coming a new vision of God, which will radically transform the reverent student. In it all seek to acquire *the historical sense*. That is, step back and see what this thing or that meant to these men as it was first spoken under their immediate circumstances.

And so push on into the New Testament. Do not try so much to fit the four Gospels into one connected story, dovetailing all the parts, but try rather to get a clear grasp of Jesus' movements those few years as told by these four men. Fit

Paul's letters into the book of Acts the best you can.

You see at once that this is a method not for a month, nor for a year, but for years. The topical and textual study grow naturally out of it. And meanwhile you are getting an intelligent grasp of this wondrous classic, you are absorbing the finest literature in the English tongue, and infinitely better yet, you are breathing into your very being a new, deep, broad, tender conception of *God*.

4

❖

SOMETHING ABOUT GOD'S WILL IN CONNECTION WITH PRAYER

He Came to His Own

The purpose of prayer is to get God's will done. What a stranger God is in His own world! Nobody is so much slandered as He. He comes to His own, and they keep Him standing outside the door, while they peer suspiciously at Him through the crack of the hinges.

Some of us shrink back from making a full surrender of life to God. And if the real reason were known it would be found to be that we are *afraid* of God. We fear He will put something bitter in the cup or some rough thing in the road. And without doubt the reason we are afraid of God is because we don't *know* God. The great prayer of Jesus' heart that night with the eleven was "that they may *know* You, the only true God, and Jesus Christ whom You have sent" (John 17:3, emphasis added).

To understand God's will we must understand something of His character. There are five common, everyday words I want to bring you to suggest something of who God is. The first is the word *father*. "Father" stands for loving strength. A father plans, provides for, and protects his loved ones. If you will think of the finest father you ever knew that anybody ever had, think of him now. Then remember this, God is a father, only He is so much finer a father than the finest father you ever knew of. And His will for your life down here is a father's will for the one most dearly loved.

The second word is a finer word, the word *mother*. If father stands for strength, mother stands for love—great, patient, tender, enduring love. What would she not do for her loved one! Think of the finest mother you ever knew, then remember this: God is a mother, only He is so much finer a mother than the finest mother you ever knew.

The references in scripture to God as a mother are numerous. "Under His wings" is a mother figure. The mother-bird gathers her brood up under her wings to feel the heat of her body and for protection. The word *mother* is not used for God in the Bible. I think it is because with God "father" includes "mother." It takes more of the human to tell the story than of the divine. With God, all the strength of the father and all the fine love of the mother are combined in that word *father*. And His will for us is a wise, loving mother's will for the darling of her heart.

The third word is *friend*. I mean a friend who loves you for your sake only and steadfastly loves without regard for any return. If you will think for a moment of the very best friend you ever knew anybody to have, then remember this: God is a friend. Only He is ever so much better a friend than the best friend you ever knew of. And the plan He has thought out for your life is such a one as that word would suggest.

The fourth word I almost hesitate to use. The hesitancy is because the word and its relationship are spoken of lightly. I mean that rare fine word *lover*, where two have met and acquaintance has deepened into friendship, and that in turn into the holiest emotion, the highest friendship. What would he not do for her! She becomes the new human center of his life. In a good sense he worships the ground she walks on. And she will leave wealth for poverty to be with him in the coming days. She will leave home and friends and go to the ends of the earth if his service calls him there. Think of the finest lover, man or woman, you ever knew anybody to have, then remember this—and let me say it in reverent tones—God is a lover. Only He is so much finer a lover than the finest lover you ever knew of. And His will, His plan for your life and mine is a lover's plan for his only loved one.

The fifth word is this fourth word spun a finer degree: *husband*. This is the word on the man side for the most hallowed relationship of earth. This is the lover relationship in its perfection stage. With men husband is not always a finer word than lover. The more's the pity. In God's thought a husband is a lover *plus*. He is all that the finest lover is, and more: more tender, more eager, more thoughtful. Two lives are joined and begin living one life. Two wills, yet one. Two persons, yet one purpose. Duality in unity. Call to mind for a moment the best husband you ever knew any woman to have, then remember that God is a husband; only He is an infinitely more thoughtful husband than any you ever knew. And His will for your life is a husband's will for his life's friend and companion.

Now please don't take one of these words and

say, "I like that." How we whittle God down to our narrow conceptions! You must take all five words and think the finest meaning into each, and then put them all together to get a close-up idea of God. He is all that, *and more*.

God's will for us is the plan of such a God as that. It includes the body; the family and home matters; money and business matters; friendships, including the choice of life's chief friend; service; constant guidance; the whole life, and the world of lives.

The One Purpose of Prayer
Now, the whole thought in prayer is to get the will of a God like that done in our lives and upon this old earth. The greatest prayer anyone can offer is "Your will be done." It will be offered in a thousand different forms, with a thousand details, as needs arise daily. But every true prayer comes under those four words. There is not a good, desirable thing that you have thought of that He has not thought of first, and probably with an added touch not in your thoughts. Not to grit your teeth and lock your jaw and pray for grace to say, "Your will be *endured*; it is bitter, but I must be resigned." Not that, please. Do not slander God like that. There is a superficial

idea among men that charges God with many misfortunes and ills for which He is not at all responsible. He is continually doing the very best that can be done under the circumstances for the best results. He has a bad mixture of stubborn, warped human wills to deal with. With infinite patience and skill and diplomacy and success, too, He is ever working at the tangled skein of human life, through the human will.

It may help us here to remember that God has a first and a second will for us: a first choice and a second. He always prefers that His first will be accomplished in us. But where we will not be wooed up to that height, He comes down to the highest level we will come up to and works with us there. For instance, God's first choice for Israel was that He Himself should be their king. There was to be no human, visible king, as with the surrounding nations. He was to be their king. They were to be set apart in this. But to Samuel's sorrow and yet more to God's, they insisted upon a king. And so God gave them a king. David, the great shepherd-psalmist-king, was a man after God's own heart, and the world's Savior came of the Davidic line. God did His best upon the level they chose and a great best it was. Yet the human king and line of kings was not God's first will but a second will yielded to because the first would not be accepted. God is ever doing the best for human lives that can be done through the human will.

His first will for our bodies, without doubt, is that each of us have a strong, healthy body. But there is a far higher thing being aimed at in us than that. And with keen pain to His own heart, He often permits bodily weakness and suffering because in the conditions of our wills only can these higher things be gotten at. And where the human will comes into intelligent touch with Himself and the higher can so be reached, with great gladness and eagerness the bodily difficulty is removed by Him.

There are two things, at least, that modify God's first will for us: first of all, the degree of our intelligent willingness that He will have full sway, and second, the circumstances of one's life. Each of us is the center of an ever-changing circle of people. If we are in touch with Him, God is speaking through each of us to our circle. His dealings with us under varying circumstances are a part of His message to that circle. God is trying to win people. It takes marvelous diplomacy on His part, and God is a wondrous tactician. But—I say this very reverently—He is a needy

God. He needs us to help Him, each in our circle. We must be perfectly willing to have His will done; and more, we must trust Him to know what is best to do in us and with us in the circle of our circumstances. God is a great economist. He wastes no forces. Every bit is being conserved toward the great end in view.

There may be a false submission to His supposed will in some affliction, a not reaching out after *all* that He has for us. And at the other swing of the pendulum there may be a sort of *logical praying* for some desirable thing because a friend tells us we should claim it. By logical praying I mean the studying of a statement of God's Word, and possibly someone's explanation of it, and hearing or knowing how somebody else has claimed a certain thing through that statement and then concluding that therefore we should so claim. The trouble with that is that it stops too soon. Praying in the Spirit as opposed to logical praying is doing this logical thinking, *then* quietly taking all to God to learn what His will is for *you*, under your circumstances and in the circle of people whom He touches through you.

The Spirit's Prayer Room

There is a remarkable passage in Paul's Roman letter about prayer and God's will. "Likewise the Spirit also helps in our weaknesses. For we do not know what we should pray for as we ought, but the Spirit Himself makes intercession for us with groanings which cannot be uttered. Now He who searches the hearts knows what the mind of the Spirit is, because He makes intercession for the saints according to the will of God" (Romans 8:26–27).

Notice that these words connect with the previous verses ending with verse 17. Verses 18–25 are a parenthesis. As the Spirit within breathes out the "Father" cry of a child, which is the prayer-cry, so He helps us in praying. It is our infirmity that we do not know how to pray *as we ought*. There is willingness and eagerness, too, but a lack of knowledge. We don't know how. But the Spirit knows how. He is the Master-prayer. He knows God's will perfectly. He knows what best to be praying under all circumstances. And He is within you and me. He is there as a prayer-spirit. He prompts us to pray. He calls us away to the quiet room to our knees. He inclines us to prayer wherever we are. He is thinking thoughts that find no response in us. They cannot be expressed in our lips for they are not in our thinking. He prays with an intensity quite beyond the possibility of language to express. And the heart-searcher—God listening above—knows fully what this praying Spirit is thinking within me and wordlessly praying, for they are one. He recognizes His own purposes and plans being repeated in this man down on the earth by His own Spirit.

And the great truth is that the Spirit within us prays God's will. He teaches us God's will, He teaches us how to pray God's will, and He Himself prays God's will in us. Further, He seeks to pray God's will in us before we have yet reached up to where we know ourselves what that will is.

We should be ambitious to cultivate a healthy sensitivity to this indwelling Spirit. And when there comes that quick inner wooing to pray, let us faithfully obey. Even though we are not clear what the particular petition is to be, let us remain in prayer while He uses us as the conduit of His praying.

Often the best prayer to offer about some friend or some particular thing after perhaps stating the case the best we can is this: "Holy Spirit, be praying in me the thing the Father wants done. Father, what the Spirit within me is praying, that is my prayer in Jesus' name. Your will, what You are wishing and thinking, may that be fully done here."

How to Find God's Will

We should make a study of God's will. We ought to seek to become skilled in knowing His will. The more we know Him, the better will we be able to read His will intelligently.

It may be said that God has two wills for each of us or, better, there are two parts to His will. There is His will of grace and His will of government. His will of grace is plainly revealed in His Word. It is that we be saved, made holy and pure, and by and by be glorified in His presence. His will of government is His particular plan for my life. God has every life planned. The highest possible ambition for a life is to reach God's plan. He reveals that to us bit by bit as we need to know. If the life is to be one of special service, He will make that plain, and each next step He will make plain.

Learning His will here hinges upon three things: I must keep *in touch* with Him so He has an open ear to talk into. I must *delight* to do His will, *because it is His*. The third thing needs special emphasis. Many who are right on the first two stumble here: *His Word must be allowed to discipline my judgment as to Himself and His will.* Many of us stumble on number one and on number two, and a great many willing, earnest men sprawl badly when it comes to number three. The bother with these is the lack of a disciplined judgment about God and His will. If we would prayerfully *absorb* the Book, there would come a better poised judgment. We need to get a broad sweep of God's thought, to breathe Him in as He reveals Himself in this Book. The meek man—the man willing to yield his will to a higher will—will He guide in his judgment, that is, in his mental processes.

This is John's standpoint: "Now this is the confidence that we have in Him, that if we ask anything according to His will, He hears us. And if we know that He hears us, whatever we ask, we know that we have the petitions that we have asked of Him" (1 John 5:14–15). These words dovetail nicely into those already quoted from Paul in the eighth chapter of Romans. The whole supposition here is that we have learned His will about the particular matter at hand. Having gotten that footing, we go to prayer with great boldness. For if He wants a thing and I want it and we join—that combination cannot be broken.

5

❖

May We Pray with Assurance for the Conversion of Our Loved Ones?

God's Door into a Home

The heart of God hungers to redeem the world, for He gave His only Son, though the treatment He received tore that father's heart to the quick. He sent the Holy Spirit to do in men what the Son had done for them, and He placed in human hands the mightiest of all forces—prayer, that we might become partners with Him.

For that, too, He set man in the relationships of kinship and friendship. He wins men through men. Man is the goal, and he is also the road to the goal. Man is the object aimed at, and he is the conduit of approach, whether the advance be by God or by Satan. God will not enter a man's heart without his consent, and Satan *can*not. God would reach people through people, and Satan must. And so God has set us in the strongest relationship that binds people, the relationship of love, that He may touch one through another.

I have at times been asked by some earnest, sensitive people if it is not selfish to be especially concerned for one's own family, over whom the heart yearns much and the prayer offered is more tender and intense and more frequent. Well, if *you* do not pray for them, who will? Who *can* pray for them with such believing, persistent fervor as you! God has set us in the relationship of personal affection and kinship for just such a purpose. He binds us together with the ties of love that we may be concerned for each other. If there be but one in a home in touch with God, that one becomes God's door into the whole family.

Contact means opportunity, and that in turn means responsibility. The closer the contact the greater the opportunity and the greater the responsibility. Unselfishness does not mean to exclude one's self and one's own. It means right proportions in our perspective. Humility is not whipping one's self. It is forgetting one's self in the thought of others. Not only is it not selfish so to pray, it is a part of God's plan that we should so pray. I am most responsible for the one to whom I am most closely related.

A Free Agent Enslaved

One of the questions that is asked more often in this connection than any other perhaps is this: May we pray with assurance for the conversion of our loved ones? No question sets more hearts in an audience beating faster than that one. I remember speaking in a Boston church on this subject one week. At the close of the meeting a cultured Christian woman whom I knew came up for a word. She said, "I do not think we can pray like that." And I said, "Why not?" She paused a moment, and her well-controlled agitation told me how deeply her thoughts were stirred. Then she said quietly, "I have a brother. He is not a Christian. The theater, the wine, the club, the cards—that is his life. And he laughs at me. I would rather than anything else that my brother were a Christian. But I do not think I can pray positively for his conversion, for he is a free agent, is he not? And God will not save a man against his will."

I want to say to you today what I said to her. Man *is* a free agent, so far as God is concerned. *And* he is the most enslaved agent on the earth, so far as sin and selfishness and prejudice are concerned. The purpose of our praying is not to force or coerce his will; never that. It is to *free* his will of the warping influences that now twist it. It is to get the dust out of his eyes so his sight will be clear. And once he is free, able to see clearly, to balance things without prejudice, the whole probability is in favor of his using his will to choose the only right.

I want to suggest to you the ideal prayer for such a one. It is an adaptation of Jesus' own words. It may be pleaded with much variety of detail. It is this: deliver him from the evil one and work in him *Your will* for him, by Your power to Your glory, in Jesus' name. And there are three special passages upon which to base this prayer. The first is 1 Timothy 2:4, "[God] desires all men to be saved." That is God's will for your loved one. The second is 2 Peter 3:9, where it says that He is "not willing that any should perish but that all should come to repentance." That is God's will, or desire, for the one you are thinking of now. The third passage is on our side who do the praying. It tells who may offer this prayer with assurance. John 15:7 says: "If you abide in Me, and My words abide in you, you will ask what you desire, and it shall be done for you."

There is a statement of Paul's in 2 Timothy that graphically pictures this: "A servant of the Lord must not quarrel but be gentle to all, able to

teach, patient, in humility correcting those who
are in opposition, if God perhaps will grant them
repentance, so that they may know the truth,
and *that they may come to their senses and escape
the snare of the devil,* having been taken captive
by him to do his will" (2 Timothy 2:24–26,
emphasis added).

Without any doubt we may assure the conversion of those laid upon our hearts by such
praying. The prayer in Jesus' name drives the
enemy off the battlefield of the man's will and
leaves him free to choose rightly. There is one
rare exception to be noted. There may be *extreme*
instances where such a prayer may not be offered,
where the spirit of prayer is withdrawn. But such
are very rare and extreme, and the conviction
regarding that will be unmistakable beyond any
doubt.

I cannot resist sharing the conviction that there
are people in that lower, lost world who are there
because someone failed to put his life in touch with
God and pray.

Saving the Life
We cannot know a man's mental processes. It is
surely true that if in the very last half-twinkling of
an eye a person looks up toward God longingly,

that look is the turning of the will to God. And that is quite enough. God is eagerly watching with hungry eyes for the quick turn of a human eye up to Himself. Doubtless many a person has so turned in the last moment of his life when we were not conscious of his consciousness, nor aware of the movements of his outwardly unconscious subconsciousness. One may be unconscious of outer things and yet be keenly conscious toward God.

At a summer gathering this incident came to me. A man seemingly of mature mind and judgment told me of a friend of his. This friend, who was not a professing Christian, was thrown from a boat, sank two or three times, then was rescued and after some difficulty resuscitated. He shared afterward how swiftly his thoughts came as they are said to do to one in such circumstances. He thought surely he was drowning, was quiet in his mind, thought of God and how he had not been trusting Him, and in his thoughts he prayed for forgiveness. He lived afterward a consistent Christian life. This illustrates simply the possibilities open to one in his inner mental processes.

Here is surely enough knowledge to comfort many a bereft heart, and enough, too, to make us pray persistently and believingly for loved ones because of prayer's incalculable power.

Yet let us be wary of letting this influence us one bit further. The man who presumes upon such statements to resist God's gracious pleadings for his life is nothing less than a fool. And on our side, we must not fail to warn men lovingly yet plainly of the tremendous danger of delay in coming to God. A man may be so stupefied at the end of his life as to shut out of his range what has been suggested. And further, even if a man's soul be saved, he is responsible to God for his life. We want men to *live* for Jesus and win others to Him. And further, reward and honor in God's kingdom depend upon faithfulness to Him down here. Who wants to be saved by the skin of his teeth!

The great fact to have burned in deep is that we may assure the coming to God of our loved ones with their lives, as well as for their souls, if we will but press the battle.

Giving God a Clear Road for Action

Fact is more fascinating than fiction. If one could know what is going on around him, how surprised and startled he would be. If we could get *all* the facts in any one incident and have the judgment to sift and analyze accurately, what fascinating instances of the power of prayer would be disclosed.

There is a double side to the story I am about to tell: the side of the man who was changed and the side of the woman who prayed. He was almost a giant physically, keen mentally, a lawyer, and a natural leader. He had the conviction as a boy that if he became a Christian he was to preach. But he grew up a skeptic and read up and lectured on skeptical subjects. He was the representative of a district of his western home state in Congress, in his fourth term or so at this time.

The experience I am telling about came during a time that was not especially suited to meditation about God in the halls of Congress. Somehow he knew all the other skeptics who were in the lower house and they drifted together a good bit and strengthened each other by their talk.

One day as he was in his seat in the lower house, in the midst of the business of the hour, there came to him a conviction that God—the God in whom he did not believe—was right there above his head thinking about him and displeased at the way he was behaving toward

Him. And he said to himself: "This is ridiculous. I've been working too hard; confined too closely; my mind is getting morbid. I'll go get some fresh air and shake myself."

And so he did. But the conviction only deepened and intensified. Day by day it grew. And that went on for weeks, into the fourth month as I recall his words. Then he planned to return home to attend to some business matters and to attend to some preliminaries for securing the nomination for the governorship of his state. And as I understand he was close to securing the nomination.

He reached his home and had hardly gotten there before he found that his wife and two others had entered into a holy compact of prayer for his conversion and had been so praying for some months. Instantly he thought of his unwelcome Washington experience and became intensely interested. But not wishing them to know of his interest, he asked carelessly when "this thing began." His wife told him the day. He did some quick mental figuring, and he said to me, "I knew almost instantly that the day she named fit into the calendar with the coming of that impression about God's presence."

He was greatly startled. He wanted to be

thoroughly honest in all his thinking, and he said he knew that if a single fact of that sort could be established, of prayer producing such results, it carried the whole Christian scheme of belief with it. He did some stiff fighting within. Had he been wrong all those years? He sifted the matter back and forth as a lawyer would the evidence in a case. And he said to me, "As an honest man I was compelled to admit the facts, and I believe I might have been led to Christ that very night."

A few nights later he knelt at the altar in the Methodist meetinghouse in his hometown and surrendered his strong will to God. Then the early conviction of his boyhood days came back. He was to preach the Gospel. And like Saul of old, he utterly changed his life and has been preaching the Gospel with power ever since.

Then I was intensely fascinated in getting the other side, the praying side of the story. His wife had been a Christian for years, since before their marriage. But in some meetings in the home church she was led into a new, full surrender to Jesus Christ as Master, and had experienced a new consciousness of the Holy Spirit's presence and power. Almost at once came a new, intense desire for her husband's conversion. The compact of three was agreed upon, of daily prayer for him until the change came.

As she prayed that night after retiring to her room, she was in great distress of mind in thinking and praying for him. She could get no rest from this intense distress. At length she rose and knelt by the bedside to pray. As she was praying and distressed, an exquisitely quiet inner voice said, "Will you abide the consequences?" She was startled. Such a thing was wholly new to her. She did not know what it meant. And without paying any attention to it, she went on praying. Again came the same quietly spoken words to her ear, "Will you abide the consequences?" And again the half-frightened feeling. She slipped back to bed to sleep, but sleep did not come. And back again to her knees, and again the patient, quiet voice.

This time with an earnestness bearing the impress of her agony she said, "Lord, I will abide any consequence that may come if only my husband may be brought to You." And at once the distress slipped away, a sweet peace filled her being, and sleep quickly came. And while she prayed on for weeks and months patiently, persistently, day by day, the distress was gone, the sweet peace remained in the assurance that the result was surely coming. And so it was coming all those days down in the thick air of Washington's lower house, and so it did come.

What *was* the consequence to her? She had been a congressman's wife. She would likely have become the wife of the governor of her state, the first lady socially of the state. But she became a Methodist minister's wife, changing her home every few years. A very different position in many ways. No woman will be indifferent to the social difference involved. Yet rarely have I met a woman with more of that fine beauty that the peace of God brings, in her glad face and in her winsome smile.

Do you see the simple philosophy of that experience? Her surrender gave God a clear channel into that man's will. When the roadway was cleared, her prayer was a spirit force traversing instantly the hundreds of intervening miles and affecting the spirit atmosphere of his presence.

Shall we not put our wills fully in touch with God and persistently plead for each loved one, "Deliver him from the evil one, and work in him Your will, to Your glory, by Your power, in the Victor's name." And then add amen—so it *shall* be. Not so *may* it be—but so it *shall* be—an expression of confidence in Jesus' power.

IV.
Jesus' Habits
of Prayer

1

A Pen Sketch

When God wanted to win back His prodigal world He sent down a Man. That Man, while more than man, insisted upon being truly a man. He touched human life at every point. No man seems to have understood prayer as He did and to have prayed as He did. How can we better conclude these quiet talks on prayer than by gathering about His person and studying His habits of prayer?

A habit is an act repeated so often as to be done involuntarily, that is, without a new decision of the mind each time it is done.

Jesus prayed. He loved to pray. Sometimes praying was His way of resting. He prayed so much and so often that it became a part of His life. It became to Him like breathing—involuntary.

There is no thing we need so much as to learn how to pray. There are two ways of receiving instruction: one, by being told; the other, by watching someone else. The latter is the simpler and the surer way. How better can we learn how to pray than by watching how Jesus prayed and then trying to imitate Him. Not just studying what He *said* about prayer, invaluable as that is, nor yet how He received the requests of men when on earth, full of inspiring suggestion as that is of His *present* attitude toward our prayers; but how He Himself prayed when surrounded by our same circumstances and temptations.

There are two sections of the Bible to which we at once turn for light, the Gospels and the Psalms. In the Gospels is given chiefly the *outer* side of His prayer-habits; and in certain of the Psalms, glimpses of the *inner* side are unmistakably revealed.

Turning now to the Gospels, we find the picture of the praying Jesus like a sketch in black and white, the fewest possible strokes of the pen, a scratch here, a line there, frequently a single word added by one writer to the narrative of the others, which gradually bring to view the outline of a lone figure with upturned face.

Of the fifteen mentions of His praying found in the four Gospels, it is interesting to note that while Matthew gives three and Mark and John each give four, it is Luke, Paul's companion and mirrorlike friend, who, in eleven such allusions, supplies most of the picture.

Does this not contain a strong hint of the explanation of that other etching plainly traceable in the epistles that reveals Paul's own marvelous prayer-life?

Matthew, immersed in the Hebrew scriptures, writes to the Jews of their promised Davidic King; Mark, with rapid pen, relates the ceaseless activity of this wonderful Servant of the Father. John, with imprisoned body but rare liberty of vision, depicts the Son of God coming on an errand from the Father into the world, and again, leaving the world and going back home to the Father. But Luke emphasizes the *human* Jesus, a *Man*, one of ourselves. And the Holy Spirit makes it very plain throughout Luke's narrative that the *man* Christ Jesus prayed much; needed to pray; *loved* to pray.

Oh! when shall we down here, sent into the world as He was sent into the world, with the same mission, the same field, the same Satan to combat, the same Holy Spirit to empower, find out that power lies in keeping closest connection with the Sender and most complete insulation from the power-absorbing world!

2

DISSOLVING VIEWS

Let me rapidly sketch those fifteen mentions of the Gospel writers, attempting to keep their chronological order.

The first mention is in Luke 3. The first three Gospels all tell of Jesus' double baptism, but it is Luke who adds "and praying." It was while waiting in prayer that He received the gift of the Holy Spirit. He dared not begin His public mission without that anointing. It had been promised in the prophetic writings. And now, standing in the Jordan, He waits and prays until the blue above is burst through by the gleams of glory-light and the dove-like Spirit wings down and abides on Him. *Prayer brings power.* Prayer *is* power. The time of prayer is the time of power. The place of prayer is the place of power. Prayer is tightening the connections with the divine dynamo so that the power may flow freely without loss or interruption.

The second mention is made by Mark in chapter 1. Luke, in chapter 4, hints at it: "When it was day, He departed and went into a deserted place" (Luke 4:42). But Mark tells us plainly, "In the morning, having risen a long while before daylight [or, a little more literally, 'very early while it was yet very dark'], He went out and departed to a solitary place; and there He prayed" (Mark 1:35). The day before, a Sabbath day spent in His adopted hometown Capernaum, had been a very busy day for Him, teaching in the synagogue service, the interruption by a demon-possessed man, the casting out amid a painful scene; afterward the healing of Peter's mother-in-law, and then at sunset the great crowd of diseased and demonized thronging the narrow street until far into the night, while He, passing among them, by personal touch, healed and restored every one. It was a long and exhausting day's work. One of us spending as busy a Sabbath would probably feel that the next morning needed an extra hour's sleep if possible. One must rest surely. But Jesus seemed to have another way of resting in addition to sleep. Probably He occupied the guest-chamber in Peter's home. The house was likely astir at the usual hour, and by and by breakfast was ready, but the Master has not appeared yet, so they wait a bit. After a while the maid slips to His door and taps lightly, but there is no answer; again a little bolder knock, then pushing the door ajar she finds the room unoccupied. Where's the Master? "Ah!" Peter says; "I think I know. I have noticed before this that He has a way of slipping off early in the morning to some quiet place where He can be alone." And a little knot of disciples with Peter in the lead starts out on a search for Him, for already a crowd is gathering at the door and filling the street again, hungry for more. They track Him down on the hillsides, coming upon Him quietly praying with a wondrous calm in His great eyes. Listen to Peter as he eagerly blurts out, "Master, there's a big crowd down there, all asking for You." But the Master's quiet, decisive tones reply, "Let us go into the next towns that I may preach there also; for to this end came I forth."

Much easier to go back and deal again with the old crowd of yesterday; harder to meet the new crowds with their new skepticism. But there's no doubt about what *should* be done. Prayer wonderfully clears the vision; steadies the nerves; defines duty; stiffens the purpose; sweetens and strengthens the spirit. The busier the day for Him the more surely must the morning appointment be kept, and even an earlier start made, apparently. The more virtue went forth from Him, the more certainly must He spend time, and even *more* time, alone with Him who is the source of power.

The third mention is in Luke 5. Not a great while after the scene just described, He had healed a badly diseased leper, who, disregarding His express command, so widely published the fact of His remarkable healing that great crowds blocked Jesus' way in the village and compelled Him to go out to the country district, where the crowds thronged about Him. Now note what the Master does: "He Himself often withdrew into the wilderness and prayed" (Luke 5:16). A more nearly literal reading would be, "He was retiring in the deserts and praying," suggesting not a single act but rather *a habit of action* running through several days or even weeks. That is, being compelled by the greatness of the crowds to go into the deserts or country and districts and being constantly thronged there by the people, He had *less opportunity* to get alone, and yet more need, and so while He patiently continued His work among them He studiously sought opportunity to retire at intervals from the crowds to pray.

How much His life was like ours. Pressed by

duties, by opportunities for service, by the great need around us, we are strongly tempted to give less time to the inner chamber. "Surely this work must be done," we think, "though it does crowd our prayer time some." *No*, the Master's practice here says with intense emphasis. Not work first and prayer to bless it. But the *first* place given to prayer, and then the service growing out of such prayer will be charged with unmeasured power. The greater the outer pressure on His closet-life, the more jealously He guarded against either a shortening of its time or a flurrying of its spirit. The tighter the tension, the more time must there be for unhurried prayer.

The fourth mention is found in Luke 6. "It came to pass in those days that He went out to the mountain to pray, and continued all night in prayer to God" (6:12). The time is probably about the middle of the second year of His public ministry. He had been having very exasperating experiences with the national leaders from Judea who dogged His steps, criticizing and nagging at every turn, sowing seeds of skepticism among His simpleminded, intense-spirited Galileans. It was also the day *before* He selected the twelve disciples and preached the mountain sermon. Luke does not say that He *planned* to spend the entire night in prayer. Wearied in spirit by the ceaseless petty picking and satanic hatred of His enemies, thinking of the serious work of the morrow, there was just one thing for Him to do. He knew where to find rest and sweet fellowship, a calming presence and wise counsel. Turning His face northward, He sought the solitude of the mountain not far off for quiet meditation and prayer. And as He prayed and listened, daylight gradually grew into twilight, and that yielded imperceptibly to the brilliant stars spraying down their lustrous firelight. And still He prayed, while the darkness below and the blue above deepened and the calm of God wrapped around all nature and hushed His heart into a deeper peace. In the fascination of the Father's loving presence He was utterly lost to the flight of time but prayed on and on until, by and by, the earth had once more completed its daily turn, the gray streaks of dawn crept up the east, and the face of Palestine was kissed by a sun of a new day. And then, "when it was day, He called His disciples to Himself; and from them He *chose* twelve. . . . And a great multitude of people. . .came. . . . And they were healed. . . ." And He opened His mouth and taught them, "*for power went out from Him*" (Luke 6:13, 17–19, emphasis added). Is it any wonder, after such a night! If all our exasperations and embarrassments were followed, and all our decisions and utterances preceded, by unhurried prayer, what power would come forth from us, too. Because as He is even so are we in this world.

The fifth mention is made by Matthew in chapter 14, and Mark in chapter 6, John hinting at it in chapter 6 of his Gospel. It was about the time of the third passover, the beginning of His last year of service. Both He and the disciples had been kept exceedingly busy with the great throng coming and going incessantly. The startling news had just come of the tragic death of His forerunner. There was need of bodily rest, as well as of quiet to think over the rapidly culminating opposition. So taking a boat, they headed toward the eastern shore of the lake. But the eager crowds watched the direction taken and, spreading the news, literally ran around the head of the lake, and when He stepped from the boat for the much-needed rest, there was an immense company waiting for Him. Did some feeling of impatience break out among the disciples that they could not be allowed a little leisure? Very likely, for they were so much like us. But *He* was "moved with compassion" and, wearied though He was, patiently spent the entire day in teaching, and then, in the evening when the disciples proposed sending them away for food, He, with a handful of loaves and fishes, satisfied the bodily cravings of as many as five thousand.

At once it is proposed by a popular uprising to throw off the oppressive Roman yoke under the leadership of this wonderful man as king. Certainly if His consent could be had it would be immensely successful, they thought. It was a temptation, even though it found no response within Him. With the over-awing power of His presence, He quieted the movement, sent the disciples to go by boat before Him to the other side while He dismissed the throng. "And when He had sent the multitudes away, He went up on the mountain by Himself *to pray*" (Matthew 14:23, emphasis added). A second night spent in prayer! Weary in body, His spirit startled by an event that vividly foreshadowed His own approaching violent death, and now this vigorous renewal of His old temptation, again He had recourse to His one unfailing habit of getting off alone to pray. More time to pray was His one invariable offset to all difficulties, all temptations, and all needs. How much more there must have been in prayer as He understood and practiced it than many of His disciples today know.

3

❖

Deepening Shadows

We will perhaps understand better some of the remaining prayer incidents if we remember that Jesus is now in the last year of His ministry, the acute state of His experiences with the national leaders preceding the final break. The awful shadow of the cross grows deeper and darker across His path. The hatred of the opposition leader gets constantly more intense. The conditions of discipleship are more sharply put. The inability of the crowds, the disciples, and others to understand Him grows more marked. Many followers go back. He seeks more intimate time with the twelve. He makes frequent trips to distant points on the border of the outside, non-Jewish world. The coming scenes and experiences seem never absent from His thoughts.

The sixth mention is made by Luke in chapter 9. They are up north in the neighborhood of the Roman city of Cæsarea Philippi. "And it happened, as He was alone praying, that His disciples joined Him" (9:18). Alone, so far as the multitudes are concerned, but seeming to be drawing these twelve nearer to His inner life. Some of these later incidents seem to suggest that He was trying to woo them into something of the same love for the fascination of secret prayer that He had. How much they would need to pray in the coming years when He was gone. Possibly, too, He yearned for a closer fellowship with them. He loved human fellowship, and there is no fellowship among men to be compared with fellowship *in prayer*.

The seventh mention is in this same ninth chapter of Luke and records a third night of prayer. Matthew and Mark also tell of the transfiguration scene, but it is Luke who explains that He went up into the mountain *to pray*, and that it was *as He was praying* that His countenance was altered. Without stopping to study the purpose of this marvelous manifestation of His divine glory to the chosen three at a time when desertion and hatred were so marked, it is enough now to note the significant fact that it was while *He was praying* that the wondrous change came. *Transfigured while praying!* And by His side stood one who centuries before on the earth had spent so much time alone with God that the glory-light of that presence transfigured *his* face. A shining face caused by contact with God! Shall not we, to whom the Master has said, "follow Me," get alone with Him and His blessed Word so habitually that, mirroring the glory of His face, we will more and more come to bear His very likeness upon our faces? (See 2 Corinthians 3:18.)

The eighth mention is in the tenth chapter of Luke. He had organized a band of men, sending them out in twos into the places He expected to visit. They had returned with a joyful report of the power attending their work; and standing in their midst, His own heart overflowing with joy, He looked up and, as though the Father's face was visible, spoke out to Him the gladness of His heart. He seemed to be always conscious of His Father's presence, and the most natural thing was to speak to Him. They were always within speaking distance of each other, and always on speaking terms.

The ninth mention is in the eleventh chapter of Luke, very similar to the sixth mention: "It came to pass, as He was praying in a certain place, when He ceased, that one of His disciples said to Him, 'Lord, teach us to pray'" (11:1). Without